Walking with
JAMES MARTIN, SJ

Walking with
JAMES MARTIN, SJ

A Contemporary Spiritual Journey

Robert Waldron

Paulist Press
New York / Mahwah, NJ

Cover design by Sharyn Banks
Top cover image courtesy of iStockphoto.com/Stephen Strathdee
Book design by Lynn Else

Library of Congress Cataloging-in-Publication Data

Waldron, Robert G.
    Walking with James Martin, SJ : a contemporary spiritual journey / Robert Waldron.
        p. cm.
    ISBN 978-0-8091-4778-6 (alk. paper) — ISBN 978-1-61643-668-1
    1. Martin, James, S.J. 2. Jesuits—United States—Biography. I. Title.
    BX4705.M41243W35 2012
    271'.53—dc23
    [B]

                                                    2012010938

Published by Paulist Press
997 Macarthur Boulevard
Mahwah, New Jersey 07430

www.paulistpress.com

Printed and bound in the
United States of America

Contents

Dedicated to Margaret C. Waldron

Acknowledgment and Author's Note

I would like to acknowledge Sandra Walter for her research and for her reading of my manuscript.

As this is a diary, there are references to my own life, but they are few and far between. I also refer to events occurring in the world, but most of the diary is focused on the life and work of James Martin, SJ. I, however, claim the right to have opinions that are not against the teaching of the church, thus unorthodox.

Introduction

Books become best sellers, some contend, more by word of mouth than by marketing and advertising. I first heard about James Martin, SJ, from a friend who praised him while simultaneously comparing him to Thomas Merton and Henri Nouwen, two writers I have long admired, having written several books about each of them.

On reading my first book by Martin, I immediately knew that his books would take their place on my bookshelves beside those of Merton and Nouwen, for I prefer to have my favorite books within arm's length. What initially piqued my interest and attention was Martin's writing style, more like Nouwen's than Merton's—simple, accessible, and transparent. His writing would appeal to the general reader as well as the more educated. Like Nouwen, Martin is completely himself in his books. This is not to say Merton was not himself, but Merton always kept a distance between himself and his readers, revealing minimal intimacy (his now-published love for his nurse an instance of rare intimacy). Martin is completely upfront, openly and frankly sharing himself with his readers—or so is *my* conclusion.

Nevertheless, it was Merton, not Nouwen, who had the greatest influence on Martin. In fact, Merton served as his spiritual mentor; his effect on Martin's life was profound and lasting, and one that ultimately led him into the religious life. For instance, when Martin first read about Merton's concept of the True Self, it shook the very foundations of his life.

Martin, a graduate of the prestigious Wharton School of Business, easily found a job in corporate America. In short time he was making money and experiencing the American Dream, but he was not happy, a sense of meaninglessness clouding his life. He had never forgotten his first reading of Thomas Merton's autobiography, remembering that Merton, too, was haunted by a feeling that there had to be more to life than a good job, partying, and drinking.

Martin was struck to the quick by a line from Merton's *No Man Is an Island*, "Every one of us is shadowed by an illusory person: the false self." Martin gradually realized that being successful in corporate America (a highly skilled accountant, also responsible for hiring and training at General Electric) was not true to the kind of person he really was. He began to read more of Merton, and he started seriously to consider his Catholicism. He had always been a lukewarm Catholic, ignorant of many of its rituals, prayers, saints, and theology. Merton's example spurred him not only to begin to better understand his faith but also to strip away false masks he had for too long been wearing and to discover his True Self. He finally realized that his search for his True Self was essentially a search for God, a realization leading him into religious life. He entered the Jesuit novitiate when he was twenty-eight. (Merton was twenty-seven when he entered the Trappists.)

Martin admits, however, to being shamefully uninformed about his Catholic faith. It may sound strange to many Catholics, particularly baby boomers, that Martin had never heard of Merton until he watched a documentary on a local PBS station. Again, Martin is the first to confess his ignorance of so much that is Catholic, but to be fair, his lack of knowledge about his faith quickly disappeared when he became a Jesuit novice.

Under the tutelage of the Jesuits, who many consider among the world's best educators, Martin began to flourish. He took to heart that to be faithful to his True Self, he would have to offer his life completely to God. He was able to do so because he always held before

2

himself the example of Thomas Merton, who gave up everything for God Alone, and the reward of it was a rich, deep, intimate life with God. Thus, Martin's joining one of the most rigorous of Catholic religious orders turned out to be the best decision of his life.

It was not, of course, an easy life. It involved much study and much work. It also required his involvement in social service. He was assigned to Africa to work with the missionaries who cared for the poor. At first, he felt useless, having no skills with which to help the poor Africans whom he was appointed to assist both physically and spiritually. When he learned about Kenyans trying to support themselves by selling wares they had made with their own hands, Martin was inspired to help them form their own small companies. He put to use all that he had learned at the Wharton School of Business and in corporate America. Not only were the lives of poor Kenyans transformed but also Martin's life. For the first time, he understood Christ's dictum, "In losing yourself you will find yourself." He had offered himself to the poor, and they helped him find his True Self, which meant for him a life of giving, not taking, strengthening his decision to enter the Jesuit novitiate, with priesthood his purpose.

After reading about Martin's experiences in Africa, I knew he was a man after my own heart, and I wanted to know as much about him as I could; thus began my search for every book he had ever written. As he had come late to Merton, I had come late to him, but as with St. Augustine, it is better to be late than never (recall Augustine's "Late Have I Loved Thee, O Beauty Ever Ancient"—to become one of Martin's favorite quotes).

At the time I first read Martin, I had not been a subscriber to the Jesuit weekly *America*. Martin was (and is) one of its editors and contributors. He had already, unbeknownst to me, several best-selling books. Knowing that he was also affiliated with *America*, I then real-

3

ized that Martin was positioned to don the mantle of Thomas Merton, able to become an important, influential Catholic voice in America. He certainly has the educational background, the intelligence, and writing talent to assume a role once held by such a varied group as Fulton Sheen, Thomas Merton, Henri Nouwen, and even Dorothy Day. In short, he is a writer that Catholics (and of course all Christians) should embrace because he indeed has important insights to share about modern spirituality. He is a writer who speaks, not from a theoretical perspective, but from lived experience. Martin, however, shares not only his experiences but also his heart.

Thus, I have chosen him to be my "walking with" companion. I already know what some of our conversations will entail. He will repeat the importance of knowing my True Self. He will emphasize that we are likely to find Jesus more in serving people than in any other way. He will encourage me not to give up in becoming who I am: by this he means not just being faithful to my True Self, but being faithful to the Christ within me.

It is my hope that you, my readers, will enjoy my walk with Martin and that you will want to know him more intimately by reading his books. Nevertheless, whether or not you ever read his books, you will have at least met a man, a priest, whom you will never forget.

Now, let us again embark on yet another leisurely "walk" with a person who may indeed transform your life.

I

Today it's seven degrees outside, but with the windchill factor, it's likely below zero. Usually I would begin writing my "Walking With" books in the summer. From September to June, I was busy teaching, reading, and correcting mounds of students' papers, but now that I'm retired, I have more time for writing.

I've just finished two books for Paulist: *Walking with Gerard Manley Hopkins* and *The Wounded Heart of Thomas Merton*. And this week, on Wednesday, my novella about Hopkins, *The Secret Dublin Diary of Gerard Manley Hopkins*, will be published in Ireland, and shortly in the United Kingdom. So retirement has gifted me with precious time to write, and I must admit I'm enjoying it immensely.

In the past, I would usually choose a walking partner with whom I was very familiar but about whom I wished to know more. This time, however, I know little about Father James Martin. I know who he is, but to be honest I have read few of his books, many of which are best sellers. I've read his columns in *America* where he's still an editor, but if I had to describe my relationship with him as of now, I'd have to say we're merely acquaintances. I hope by the end of writing this book, we will have become friends.

Some people might think it odd that I refer to writers I like or admire as "friends." It initially sounds odd, but because books are so much a part of my life, they actually affect the way I think, and more importantly the way I live. Some books have saved me from depression, others from despair. So, in my gratitude for the inspirational power of books, I now consider their authors my "friends."

There are, I should add, certain books that I often reread, books I go to when I need them just as I would call a friend when I need someone to talk with if I'm blue or need advice through a difficult time. I'm not apologizing for my attitude toward books, just acknowledging my heartfelt gratitude for them.

On that note, I have been blessed to receive notes and a few rather long letters from people who say *my* books have helped them in their lives. To receive such a note or letter is a great grace, for if I can reach and perhaps inspire one person, my book's existence is confirmed and verified. It then makes no difference if the book is a commercial success or makes any money (although my publishers certainly don't think this way!). In fact, I've never written anything for money. All my books have been labors of love. In this case, however, I cannot say this book is a labor of love because I don't know much about James Martin, but I suspect that by the end of writing it, I'll be glad to have "walked" with him. This isn't mere speculation because I've just finished reading one of his books, and I immediately know that in matters of spirituality, we're on the same wavelength, and it will be a joy to get to know my new "walking with" friend.

I'm rereading Martin's *Becoming Who You Are: Insights on the True Self from Thomas Merton and Other Saints.* This is the first Martin book I have ever read, and I'm so happy I have begun my acquaintance (and hopefully friendship) with it because it's such an accessible book. I admire his writing style; it reminds me of Father Nouwen's transparent writing style, one that makes itself accessible to readers. Nouwen intuitively understood that to reach more people he had to write as if he were talking one-on-one with his reader, for after reading one of his books, one departs feeling that he has had an authentic encounter with Father Nouwen, as if he were actually speaking to you.

I feel the same way about Martin. He had me in the palm of his hand with the first line of his Introduction: "For me to be a saint means to be myself," wrote the Trappist monk Thomas Merton in his book *New Seeds of Contemplation.* As I am, Martin is a great admirer of Thomas Merton, so right from the beginning we're in lockstep. To quote that particular line from Merton is an example of synchronicity: I was very moved when I first read it many years ago—it freed me from wanting to be a saint. A saint, as presented by well-meaning nuns and priests, lived on his or her knees and was holy beyond words and as perfect as our heavenly Father is perfect. To be told, however, that to be a saint meant *being yourself* was a revolutionary idea. This concept obviously moved Martin too. It was a good harbinger that we'd walk well together.

Like Merton, Martin was not from a particularly religious family. His father would drive him and his sister to Sunday Mass, but he remained in the car, reading the Sunday paper. His father once said, "I've been to Mass enough for one lifetime....When you're an adult you can stop going to Mass, too." I like the honesty of Martin's brief story because it reveals a man who isn't layered in masks, a theme about which Merton often wrote. Merton had to strip himself of many masks before he discovered his True Self, a concept that Martin immediately embraces, a sign that not only does he know Merton well, but that he has pierced to the heart of his message.

As a high school student, Martin wasn't a particularly spiritual young man. He went to Mass a few times a month, but eventually even that tapered off. Spiritual practices like the Rosary, the

Eucharist, and prayer began to appear silly to him. There was no indication in his high school years that he would someday become a Jesuit. Again, he's more like Merton than Nouwen: no one who knew Merton as a teenager would have imagined a religious life for him. It was quite the opposite for Nouwen; everyone in his family and all his friends knew he yearned to be a priest from early childhood. In fact, his favorite "game" as a boy was to play priest. He even had an altar and wore vestments provided for him by his grandmother!

Father Martin attended the University of Pennsylvania where he began to attend Mass more and prayed, his prayers usually requests for things, like a good grade in a course. Priesthood was definitely not on the horizon. He, in fact, enrolled in the Wharton School of Business at Penn, majoring in finance, a subject at which he was quite gifted.

He seems just to have fallen into being a business major. He wasn't asking the real, big questions: "Do you like what you're doing?" or "What do you want to do for a career?" Or the most important question of all, "Who do you want to *be*?"

How many hundreds if not thousands of students like Martin did I come across? Many times, I'd ask my senior students what they wanted to be when they "grew up," by which I meant what profession interested them as a lifetime pursuit. I was always amazed that most of them didn't have a clue about what they wanted to do or to become in life.

I knew in grammar school that I wanted to be either a priest or a teacher. I had no doubt that I would end up being one. The background of my decision is that I wanted a job (Catholics prefer the word *vocation*) that involved people; I wanted to help them live, to be of service to them (perhaps I was presumptuous, but being a young

8

Catholic, I was idealistic). I wasn't concerned in the least with money. Nevertheless, my students wanted jobs (*that* they knew!) that "made a lot of money."

I sometimes think my generation, that of the Peace Corps, was more altruistic than the generation that came after the cultural revolution of the 1960s, but it's likely unfair to today's kids, who reflect the culture in which they've been raised. I'm sure they care about the world as much as we did, but for various reasons they haven't been able to connect with their ideals. Perhaps the state of today's world has rendered them more cynical.

Martin entered the business world after graduation. He made good money, but he felt miserable, constantly questioning the meaning of his life. By coincidence (is there such a thing?), he went home one night and turned on TV and found a documentary devoted to the life of Thomas Merton, about whom he knew nothing. Merton mesmerized him: he found him brilliant, funny, holy, and unique. The TV program inspired him to purchase Merton's autobiography, *The Seven Storey Mountain*. This book "captivated" him as no other book ever had.

Regarding Merton, both Martin and I have shared the same experience: we were not the same persons after reading this awe-inspiring autobiography—we along with how many hundreds of thousands?

I'm so pleased that Martin and I hold Merton's *No Man Is an Island* in high esteem. Scholars, and Merton himself, rate *New Seeds of Contemplation* as the better book, but Martin and I seem to have a soft spot for "No Man," which, in my opinion, is vastly underrated. Martin describes it as a book that catches Merton "thinking aloud."

Merton chose to create this impression for his readers, but as with all his books, it's a scrupulously crafted pose. It's the reason I always say that of the two writers, Merton and Nouwen, the latter is the more "naked" or transparent writer. Merton in his published books is as scrupulously adroit as a painter arranging a still life before painting.

Flipping through *No Man Is an Island* (title from a John Donne meditation), Martin comes across a passage that we of the 1960s would say "blew his mind":

> Why do we have to spend our lives striving to be something we would never want to be?

Martin instantly perceives that the question piercingly applies to himself, to his life, a question he was unable to articulate for himself either out of unconscious repression or out of fear of its possible ramifications.

How often in our lives do we avoid introspection because we don't want to face those personal aspects about ourselves that truly matter? We keep ourselves overly busy and living habitually, avoiding at all cost solitude and silence, the two states of being that foster self-reflection, or we, in Freudian fashion, quickly repress all that we find is too close to the truth of our lives: a truth we can't bear to face for it would demand change in our lives.

For Martin, Merton's question is an "Aha!" moment in his life. He realizes that he is indeed striving toward something he doesn't want to be: a businessman. Thus, the question is a life-transitional one, or, as Jung might describe it, a midlife-crisis question. What is certain is that it forced Martin to take stock of his life, and it became overtly apparent that he was not at all happy at what he was doing.

Like Merton, whose life was forever transformed after reading Etienne Gilson's *The Spirit of Medieval Philosophy*, Martin's life changed, and he began to ponder becoming a priest, in particular a Jesuit priest. This idea of priesthood appears seemingly out of the blue, after six years of corporate life. Two years after reading Merton, Martin applied for entry into the Jesuit novitiate and was accepted.

The salient difference between Merton's and Martin's lives is that Merton was a convert to Catholicism and Martin a cradle Catholic. What they share is the powerful influence of a book, for Merton one by Etienne Gilson and for Martin one by Thomas Merton.

I've never underestimated the power of books to change one's life because my life has been influenced greatly by the writings of others. Some of them are Merton, Fulton Sheen, Henri Nouwen, Simone Weil, Paul Tillich, and Iris Murdoch's fiction. I shudder to think of a life without books. I'm astonished that today's young people haven't much regard for books, preferring instead their iPods and other electronic gadgets. I'm surely just not "with it" any longer and must accept my status as a dinosaur.

Merton had toyed with the idea of joining several religious orders and finally settled on the Franciscans. They accepted him but rescinded their acceptance when they discovered that he had fathered a child out of wedlock, which in a burst of scrupulous guilt, Merton confessed to them. There was no need to inform them, but in the end, his decision proved fortuitous, for the Trappists gladly accepted him, even after learning about his transgressions. I now can't help wondering if any Catholic religious order today would accept Merton as a postulant. My gut says no. What a tragedy it would be! Certainly today, many a gifted, sincere, pious young man has indeed been rejected after telling the truth about his past or the truth about his sexual orientation. Seminaries, although they haven't literally done so, have figuratively over their doors "Gays need not apply." Sad.

Martin seems not to have had to wring his hands about which order to join. He seemingly glides into the decision-making process,

11

stating quite simply that God, not he, made the decision for him to join the Jesuits.

There is something not only simple about his decision but also impressively authentic. He humbly says that his inner voice spoke to him, telling him what to do. He names this voice the "Great Problem Solver": God.

His narration about becoming a priest is refreshing. How many autobiographies and memoirs have I read over the years with reams of pages devoted to the "life-transforming" decision that could have been described in a sentence or two, but the writer has chosen to render it as grand opera or rather soap opera.

Merton's autobiography is an exception. If you read it carefully, he is quite stark about his conversion experience (and about his decision to become a priest). He was in his room reading Lahey's biography of Gerard Manley Hopkins, and when he came to the section about Hopkins's acceptance into the church by John Henry Newman, he quickly shut the book and headed to Corpus Christi Church to find out how to become a Catholic. The whole event is narrated in Hemingway-like prose: austere, brief, and to the point. In this fashion, Merton would continue to write all his life. It's one of the reasons, in my opinion, that he's still so popular: his writing style is accessible to everyone, to the general reader as well as scholars.

Martin's writing style is also accessible, and it's surely one of the reasons his books sell so well.

Such life-transforming decisions (Merton's conversion or Martin's becoming a priest) don't actually happen in a moment. The important questions of our life are often percolating in our subconscious minds without our knowing it; we are, on a deep level of ourselves, already struggling with important life issues. The subconscious has ways to make us aware of them: we are sometimes informed by our dreams, or by sudden and unpredictable depression, or by feelings of emptiness and lack of purpose. We can ignore these signs by repressing them even deeper into the subconscious or we can address them by bringing them into the light of consciousness.

A book or a poem can indeed help these important issues to rise into our consciousness, as it did with Martin. Merton had articulated in *No Man Is an Island* the question that Martin was unable at the time to articulate for himself. Thus, when he read Merton, it wasn't difficult (or a shock) for him to see himself in the mirror of Merton's writing, which is the hallmark of a great writer: one who helps us to see ourselves as we really are.

II

After writing my previous entry, I returned to Martin's book to find him referring again to *No Man Is an Island*; he considers seriously another of Merton's insights, "We cannot become ourselves unless we know ourselves." This insight is, of course, the heart of Merton's life-long message, one that I too took to heart when I first read *No Man Is an Island*. And because of Merton, Martin commences his quest to know himself. It's an age-old but ever-new theme, one the Greeks carved into the stone of their temples: "Know Thyself."

Later, while reading Merton's *New Seeds of Contemplation*, Martin again recognizes himself in another of Merton's piercing insights: "Every one of us is shadowed by an illusory person: the false self." This perception hits home because Martin has assumed the *persona* (mask) of the businessman. But the mask he has chosen has nothing to do with his True Self. He's playacting in his profession, and he knows it.

He's intrigued by the idea of the True Self, like the face being bandaged in many layers as the character in *The Invisible Man*. It will take much effort to unfold the bandages that hide the True Self, but he's willing to make the effort. Why? At first, it's not out of any desire to be holy or to be a saint but because he is unhappy and hates his life.

Martin was a scribbler as many writers are. I have lots of notebooks filled with scribbles—some of them actually contain some of my best insights about myself and about life. I've saved all my scribbles. One night after work, still at his desk, a colleague happened to read one of Martin's scribbles and asked him, "Do you really hate your life?" It was an important event in his life because his mask dropped momentarily, and he stood psychologically naked before his friend. But he wasn't yet ready to own up to his unhappiness and conjured an excuse: "Oh, I was just having a bad day, you know?" As he says himself, in a moment of panic, the false self had reasserted itself.

Wearing a mask is much easier than changing ourselves!

Many of us know how Martin felt because we too wear masks. But we have a choice: we can continue to wear false masks or discard them. To rid ourselves of false masks demands arduous soul-work. Jung refers to the process of finding ourselves as *individuation*, a process whose ultimate goal is spiritual wholeness. On the very day he admitted to wearing false masks, he was on the road to individuation.

A bit more about masks. There are some people who live a lifetime without ever realizing that they are layered in them. To wear a mask isn't intrinsically evil. Jung says we all have to protect ourselves with *personae* (Latin for *masks*), or the world will maul us. Thus, the doctor who goes to hospital everyday dons his doctor mask, the teacher his teacher mask, the lawyer his lawyer mask. The problems arise when a person believes the mask is his True Self. To be unaware of our masks keeps us in the dark about who we really are. Thus, it's good practice to foster in our lives daily introspection and self-reflection.

Martin is a reader. He reads in order to understand himself, the likely reason he is drawn to a writer like Thomas Merton. Merton's raison d'être is to know himself, therefore to know God, for God abides within each of us. Seeking self-knowledge through reading is a path to God, and it can be a thrilling adventure.

Martin ends his section on Merton by quoting the famous

Louisville Vision. Everyone who reads Merton's epiphany—it occurred while he was standing on a busy intersection of Louisville, Kentucky—is moved by it. It is a high point in Merton's life because it reveals that he finally rejects the *contemptus mundi* that he brought with him into the Abbey of Gethsemani. To go from disliking (near to loathing) to loving the world is a huge leap as well as a testament to the kind of spiritually intensive life Merton led in the abbey.

If Merton's paean of love for mankind (the Louisville Vision) hadn't appeared in his writing, we all would have been in doubt about whether or not Merton had wisely chosen to become a Cistercian monk. But we have the evidence that he had chosen well for his particular needs, and even Martin recognized this fact and is moved by it.

There is no evidence in what I've read so far about Martin that he suffered from a similar malady: disliking and/or distrusting the world. In fact, he's quite honest about admitting that he was an ordinary man who enjoyed his success, parties, friends, expensive clothes, and networking. But enjoyment doesn't equal happiness, and Martin possessed sufficient self-knowledge (increased by reading Merton) to understand that there was a great deal more to life than his experience as a successful American businessman who had in effect achieved the American Dream.

III

Wonderful news from Ireland! My novel *The Secret Dublin Diary of Gerard Manley Hopkins* will be discussed on the Irish popular cultural program *The View*. My editor has informed me that this is a coup because the program usually reviews only books of renowned writers. I'm far from renowned, so I'm quite excited. As with all books, only time will tell if it will be successful, but a good review can always help (it was a mixed review, the reviewers terribly misinformed about Hopkins's life).

I thoroughly enjoyed Martin's chapter "So Who Am I, Anyway." Martin as a young novice found himself comparing himself to his peers, who appeared to be smarter, more organized, and far more holy than he. One particular novice possessed an aura of holiness that greatly impressed Martin, and he began to emulate him. It took him a while to realize that he again had assumed an inauthentic mask. How amazed he was when later this very young man admiringly said to Martin, "I wish I were as outgoing as you are!"

Martin's growth toward self-knowledge is gradual as it often is in life. Unfortunately, some people never achieve self-knowledge. When I taught *King Lear*, I emphasized to my students that King Lear's character flaw was his lack of self-knowledge. Many of them argued with me, contending that a man as old as King Lear had to know himself. I would then quote one of Lear's daughters, "He hath ever but slenderly known himself"—emphasizing the play's main theme.

Martin gradually learned to accept all aspects of himself, including the negative ones, which Jung calls the archetypal *shadow*. None of us is perfect. Martin, like so many Catholics of his time, was caught up with the Biblical dictum, "Be ye perfect as your heavenly Father is perfect." How many Catholic men and women drove themselves into spiritual turmoil trying to be perfect? As if it were even possible!

My spiritual breakthrough occurred when I read Jung's advice to a young Dominican, to whom he explained that the Greek word often interpreted as "perfect" was closer in meaning to "whole." What an "Aha!" moment it was for me. I could, with hard work, achieve wholeness. Perfection? Never.

Martin begins to accept himself, and he finds confirmation of his new self-discovery in Psalm 139, particularly in one verse: "For I am fearfully and wonderfully made." One could write a book about this one line: it underscores the uniqueness and beauty of each person. His fellow Jesuit Gerard Manley Hopkins had wisely understood this wisdom with his concept of inscape: each person and thing in the cosmos is unique and in its own way manifests divinity.

Part of his training as a novice involved working in a hospital. Martin hated hospitals, but his novice master wisely assigned him to one. At first, he felt useless, not knowing how to interact with patients. He was insecure and afraid to speak, wondering what was the right thing to say to someone who was ill.

With one patient, a woman named Rita, he assumed the role of a chaplain whose purpose was to discuss serious matters, but all she wanted to talk about was her brother, a Jesuit priest. Martin disregarded her desires and steered her back to serious talk until he eventually realized that he had again assumed a mask: he was not being himself. And by not being himself, he was forcing Rita not to be herself. In the end, self-knowledge fortunately won the day: "I will just be *me*."

18

His decision transformed his relationship with Rita, who blossomed under his attention. Martin listened to her speak from her heart about her brother, and she gradually opened up about her illness, about how she truly felt. His True Self brought out the True Self in her.

It's almost trite these days to quote Shakespeare's famous line, "To thine own self be true," but there's much wisdom in the verse. Shakespeare's genius is to have one of the most foolish and pompous characters in all of his plays, Polonius, speak the line.

Martin was far from finished with learning about the True Self. He was assigned to the Jesuit Refugee Service in Nairobi, Kenya. He felt the same way here as he had first felt in the hospital: helpless. He offered his service to one nun, but she seemingly had all the help she needed. Without any real job to do, he, on his own initiative, became involved in "income-generating activities." These efforts allowed women to sell their handmade wares; many of them were highly skilled basket makers, carpenters, quiltmakers, woodcarvers, bookbinders. He and a woman named Uta opened a "Mikono Centre," (after the Swahili word for *hands*) where Kenyans could sell their handmade wares, and to Martin's delight, the shop prospered.

What amazed Martin, who felt so useless when he first arrived, was that he had the insight to draw upon his business acumen to help the Kenyans. He shared with them his Wharton School knowledge about accounting, marketing, management, and the need for long-term investment. He found himself being true to himself: he had a God-given talent for business and the good sense to put it to use—although no one had even hinted at it before. One would think that his superiors would have considered taking advantage of his skills and education.

It occurred to Martin that, in living his life as a Christian, he would fail to be himself if he insisted on asking himself, what would St. Francis do? What would Mother Teresa do? Or what the founder of the Jesuits, St. Ignatius of Loyola, would do?

When one poses the question in the correct fashion, then it will be answered by taking into consideration all that a person is, all his fears, hopes, experiences, and talents. Thus, there is no question, only a declarative sentence: I'll do my best according to who I am.

The second modern "saint" that Martin addresses is Henri Nouwen. Again, I'm amazed how on the same wavelength we are, for I consider Merton and Nouwen the most eloquent commentators on the spiritual life during the latter part of the twentieth century.

Martin admires Nouwen for the same reasons I do: his writing is accessible, and he's honest to a fault.

Martin's favorite Nouwen book is *Genesee Diary*, also one of my favorites. After the publication of this book, Nouwen was catapulted from the second tier of spiritual writers to the first tier. Martin loves the book because it offers luminous descriptions of monastic life. It also charts Nouwen's search for *his* True Self, and this aspect of the book intrigues Martin because he himself is still seeking his True Self.

Martin praises Nouwen for his "brutal honesty" about himself. Nouwen is maskless in *Genesee Diary*, far more than Merton ever is except in one aspect of his life (more of that later). The *Genesee Diary* entries are filled with Nouwen's desire for affirmation, for affection, and for fame. He is a tremendously needy man, and he knows this about himself and candidly shares this aspect of himself with his readers.

It's risky business to be so frank about oneself, but it works with Nouwen because he's so completely himself: a flawed and wounded human being. It's as if he's saying to his reader, "If you think you're mixed up, take a good look at me because I'm a mess." We can only admire a writer who is willing to stand so humbly and "naked" before his readers.

Merton is, as I mentioned, never "naked" before his readers. He doesn't share as much of himself. He usually dons his intellectual mask and everything is spotlighted under the penetrating light of his intellect. Whereas Merton is a diarist of the mind, Nouwen is one of the heart, and there's a huge difference. I happen to like and admire both diarists, but I admit I feel closer to Nouwen, because his frail, flawed humanity moves me more than Merton's cerebral approach to, well, everything.

In comparing the two diarists, Martin finds that they share similar "virtues":

Both are honest
Both are flawed people (let's be honest and say they're both
    neurotic)
Both are seekers, forever imagining/dreaming of the ideal
    home
Both suffer from sexual dysfunction

The last item brings us to sex. During his teenage and young adulthood, Merton was never able to establish a healthy relationship with a woman. The root of this problem may lie with the early death of his mother when he was six. In his autobiography, he describes his mother as cold and distant. This feeling may have affected his future relationships with women in general. But as a monk being treated in a

21

Louisville hospital, Merton falls head over heels in love with a young nurse, Marge. This leads to a six-month affair. This is one of the few times Merton allows himself to be psychologically "naked" in his journals: the diary description of his relationship with Marge is riveting reading because Merton is more candid than ever before. Although it's painful to read about his decision to end the affair, we end up admiring him for making the right decision.

Nouwen also fell in love as an older man, but with another man. Nouwen's biographer Michael Ford confirms that Nouwen had confided his sexual orientation to his friends. Ford speculates that Nouwen may likely have demanded too much attention of his loved friend, thus the friendship came to a temporary stop. But Nouwen took it hard, experiencing a nervous breakdown. Later, the relationship was mended, but by then Nouwen had accepted the fact that in his life there could be only one love: with God.

Martin frankly admits that he wished Nouwen had written more about his love for his friend; it is a loss because it would help his readers in addressing issues like celibacy, chastity, fidelity, love, intimacy, and of course, faith.

Nouwen likely decided not to write about his sexuality because he feared a backlash from both his publishers and perhaps Catholic censors. There is no indication that Nouwen, however, had ever broken his vow of celibacy; in fact, all indications are that he faithfully kept his vow up to his death. But the question lingers: Would his reading audience have accepted him as a homosexual man? Surely that's one of the questions that must have haunted Nouwen, who in every other aspect of his life was totally candid: he held nothing back except what concerned his sexuality. I have Catholic friends who will no longer read Merton because of his affair with his nurse. Nouwen too may have lost the respect of many of his readers if they had known about his homosexuality. To me, however, with both men, it makes no difference; if anything, it shows how *human* they are, like all of us, imbued with goodness but also flawed. Yet is it fair to say that Merton was *flawed* because he fell in love or that Nouwen was *flawed* because he was homosexual?

While reading a biography of Bede Griffiths, I was amazed when this holy man admitted that he was a homosexual. He had never acted upon it, but he accepted this aspect of himself. It took great courage for him to make such a confession, for he is one of our greatest Catholic voices.

I too wish Nouwen had written more about his love for his friend Nathan Ball. I believe it would have been cathartic for him. As for readers rejecting him, well, there's always that chance any time sexuality enters the picture, but on the other hand, because his friendship remained Platonic it may not have made any difference to anyone.

With Merton, however, there are indications in his diary entries that point toward breaking his vow of chastity. I believe, however, that he somehow had to solve what he often referred to as his "problem" with women, and this was accomplished with his nurse. In the end, he remained a monk at Gethsemani.

Most people don't know that Merton considered himself unlovable. So when a beautiful, young nurse fell in love with him, he couldn't quite believe it. When reading his account of their love, I was charmed by his descriptions of himself because he's so in love he sounds like a lovesick teenager. I found myself saying, "Good for you, Tom, and now maybe you can get on with your True Self, being a Trappist monk."

As mentioned, with the hardliners I've met over the years, Merton is considered a failed monk and a failed priest. But it's not for us to judge. Judgment should be left to Christ who forgave Peter, who denied him three times, and if Christ can forgive those who nailed him to the cross, who are we not to be compassionate toward Merton?

What it finally comes down to is that Merton and Nouwen in the end were true to themselves. And for Martin that's what counts, for he again reminds his readers that for him everything finally rises to this point—and here he employs Merton's rather than his own words, "For me to be a saint means to be myself."

We cannot escape the world or the cosmos. We surely cannot escape ourselves (if we try to, we are miserably unhappy). In fact, rather than escape ourselves, we, according to Martin, must learn *who we are* and simultaneously accept and love ourselves. It's easy to say, he admits, but difficult to do.

At the end of his book, Martin mentions other modern saints: Dorothy Day, Flannery O'Connor, Mother Teresa, Bernadette of Lourdes, and others. He's seemingly fascinated with Mother Teresa and comments on how so many people try to emulate her in their lives. But he again makes the telling point: we cannot emulate another. We can admire others, but ultimately we can only be ourselves. And that, briefly, is the message of this inspiring, readable book: Be yourself.

IV

When I saw the title *A Jesuit, Off Broadway, Center Stage with Jesus, Judas, and Life's Big Questions* on the library shelf, I was instantly intrigued. First, I'm a theater buff (as well as a movie buff), and I was intrigued by how a Jesuit priest involved himself in off-Broadway, the testing ground not only of new playwrights and new, young, creative actors, but often the birthplace of what would become classic American plays.

I took the book home, but because of my own writing commitments, I never had the chance to read it. But, now writing a "walking with" Father Martin, I've just finished reading his enjoyable and insightful book. It's a lively, roller-coaster account of his six-month collaboration with the author of the play *The Last Days of Judas Iscariot* by Stephen Adly Guirgis and with its cast, including actors like Sam Rockwell and its director, now a famous, Academy Award-winning actor, Philip Seymour Hoffman.

When I first glimpsed the title of this book, the name of Judas jumped out at me, as well as a terrific blurb from a famous actor, Martin Sheen, who exudes, "Extraordinary revelations on theology, the priesthood, and the theater. Bravo!" Not bad. Then to learn that a play about Judas had been performed in New York, well, it was proof that I'd somehow become distant about what was happening in today's American theater. There was a time when I prided myself on the number of plays and movies that I had seen. But caring for a sick parent for over six years, I'd become far removed from what was vital and excit-

25

ing in the world of theater and movies. As to movies, although I couldn't attend them, I could always rent them at Blockbuster (alas, there are no Blockbusters left in my neighborhood). I had seen Hoffman in *Capote* (which I rented) and no doubt about it, he deserved the Academy Award. I'd seen Bobby Morse's version of Capote's life at Harvard, and it was a riveting performance; I believed no one could top it, but Hoffman's performance is as fine, if not superior.

I also admired Hoffman's work in the film *Doubt*, costarring with Meryl Streep. It, too, is a riveting play, about a priest falsely accused of pedophilia. Streep and Hoffman match each other in acting, two pros who know how to make a scene come alive, who know the importance of underplaying, for this play demands not arias but a quiet speaking of the lines, because it's a subtle play, whose meaning is to be found between the words.

I digress. Martin is offered the opportunity to act as the theological consultant of the play. If you're going to write a play about Judas, about whether or not he's been fairly judged by the world, then you need someone well versed in theology. Martin fills the bill. He's savvy, well informed, and he did his homework, reading a number of books addressing Judas and the New Testament. Of course, being a Jesuit, he was already well trained in theology, but unlike so many priests who after ordination never read another book, Martin is an inveterate reader, and I'm impressed by the amount of reading he's able to accomplish in his rather busy life as a priest, lecturer, and author.

The premise of the play is simple (at least at first sight): Is Judas guilty? Has he been fairly judged? Does he deserve to be loathed as the world's greatest traitor? Martin cites a historical study, *Judas: Images of the Lost Disciple*, by Kim Paffenroth, a religious studies professor at Iona College in New York, who says, "For Dante, Judas is the worst example of the worst sin possible, betrayal, and therefore he places him at the center of hell, the worst of human sinners." Dante, by the way, damns Judas to hell's nadir where forever a three-headed Satan devours him. Yikes!

In general, that's what the play is about: to put Judas on trial, to discover if he is indeed our worst sinner, our worst traitor. To address this proposition is an enormous undertaking. I shudder to think how much time and effort would have to go into such a play, but Guirgis isn't in the least threatened by the magnitude (or the controversy) of such a play. He's also humble enough to realize that he'll likely need someone who's a theological expert. Thus, a call is made to Father Martin, whose initial reaction was dubious to say the least. After meeting with Sam Rockwell, the actor chosen to play Judas, however, Martin was won over to serve as a consultant, although he was upfront, honestly admitting that we don't know very much about Judas. The play would not only be a challenge for its author, its director, and cast, but also for its consultant: Jesuit priest James Martin.

The image of Judas is that of a man with red hair, stingy with money, and a man with a fiery temper. Much of this portrayal is not necessarily based on the New Testament. The name of Judas may derive from the Semitic word describing a man's occupation, a red dyer. The name Iscariot may derive from the Semitic word meaning "to lie." Or it may simply refer to Judas's place of birth, a village named Kerioth in Judea.

I have always had questions about Judas's role in our salvation. What would have happened if there had been no betrayer? Someone had to do the dastardly deed. Was Judas predestined to betray Christ? We cannot accept such an explanation because as Catholics we believe in free will. But, of course, people will ask the question anyway, "Was he indeed free?" A question that gives one pause for thought....

The play's premise is a promising one. What is unusual in the opening pages of Martin's book is his kindness toward actor Sam Rockwell (Judas), who is illiterate about the New Testament. He hadn't any religious upbringing, except for a month at a Catholic grammar school. His grandmother is Irish Catholic and his mother is a practicing Catholic; she advised Rockwell to contact Martin to learn about Judas.

What Rockwell knows about Christianity he has gleaned from movies, and some of them were very fine ones: Webber's *Jesus Christ Superstar*, Zeffirelli's *Jesus of Nazareth*, and Gibson's *The Passion of the Christ*.

Here are Sam Rockwell's basic questions:

What was life like for the apostles?
What do we know about Judas Iscariot?
Why did Judas betray Jesus?
Could Jesus have forgiven him?

The most important question to me is, Why did Judas betray Jesus? Martin notes that scripture scholar William Barclay of the University of Glasgow suggests that Judas may have been trying to force Jesus to act, that is, he is the Messiah for whom the Jews have been waiting. Therefore, his first act would be to overthrow Roman rule.

Rockwell listens quietly to Martin. Then to Martin's surprise, Sam says, "Maybe Judas was throwing Jesus into the deep end of the pool, hoping he'll swim." Martin likes the analogy so much he employs it in his next homily. And Sam's insight makes its way into the play.

Rockwell is a method actor. He needs to *become* Judas, thus know-

28

ing the character's motivation is all-important. I don't know any actors, but over the years I've read much about how actors prepare themselves for their roles. I, consequently, am familiar with method acting, particularly the famous acting school in New York City founded by Lee Strasberg. Well-known actors, like Paul Newman, Montgomery Clift, Robert De Niro, Marlon Brando, Shelley Winters, even Marilyn Monroe attended the school. The gist of the method, as I understand it, is that the actor must "become" the role by allowing his own personality to disappear. This methodology sounds dangerous to me. I recall Elizabeth Taylor warning Monty Clift that after a scene you must let the role go and return to yourself or one could quickly burn out while making the movie. A movie shouldn't consume a person's identity. Her method of acting was simply to memorize the lines, do her best in the scene, and afterwards forget it. It is similar to Spencer Tracy's acting philosophy. I recall reading that he told his friend Katherine Hepburn, simply speak your lines as best as you can; as for emoting, he advised her, "Less is more."

Marlon Brando is, of course, America's most famous method actor. If his role of Stanley in *A Streetcar Named Desire* spilled over into his real life, I wouldn't have wanted to be near him!

Rockwell possesses all the hallmarks of the method actor: he needs to know all he can about Judas—his parentage, his town of birth, his occupations, his desires. He needs to know all those facts if he is going to make an audience believe in Judas. And of course to answer that most important question for any actor: What is my motivation?—he needs as much knowledge about Judas as he can garner.

Martin offers an insightful comment about Christ: Jesus chose Judas to be one of his apostles, and Jesus was a shrewd judge of character; thus, he had to have seen something good, something redeeming in Judas; otherwise, he never would have invited him to be one of his twelve apostles. Martin then says, "This alone argues for a more sympathetic portrayal of Judas." Bravo! He's willing to climb out on a limb for one of our most hated historical figures, who most people would rank with such monsters as Hitler and Stalin. But Martin is open to giving Judas a chance to prove himself innocent: it is essentially what the play is about. To Martin's credit, he accepts the role he's been offered, the play's theological advisor (and perhaps the devil's advocate?).

The play's controversial nature, I'm convinced, would have scared off most priests, afraid that the omnipresent Catholic censors would be swift to pounce on them, as they often had with Thomas Merton.

Martin offers important historical information about how Christians treated Jews throughout history. This issue must be addressed because *who* condemned Christ to crucifixion must be determined. Martin notes the controversy over Mel Gibson's play *The Passion of the Christ*. Gibson, to give him credit, tries to be fair and balanced in placing the blame for Christ's condemnation. However, after his drunken tirade about Jews, claiming that they are the cause of most of the world's problems, his "fairness" will never be taken seriously. It's a touchy subject to discuss, but I truly believe Gibson tried to be balanced. For a man who was indeed raised by a man who many consider an anti-Semite, Gibson's film is a rare accomplishment, for I've seen it several times, and I've not viewed anything in it that can be remotely described as anti-Semitic.

Thus, it will be interesting to see how Martin deals with the issue of anti-Semitism when it comes up—and it will.

In the early cast readings, the play was still being written. I find this fact amazing. As a novelist, I'd never let anyone see my work until it was finished. Although I do admit I write my fiction in the manner that Guirgis employs: allowing the story to unfold itself by letting the characters transport me to where they want me to go. However, when you assemble a whole cast, including its director, and don't have a working (that is, completed) script, well, it's a daring move to say the least. Surely movies don't work this way. Imagine a movie crew arriving at a studio with the whole cast present, including director, but there's no screenplay or only an incomplete one. The producers of the film would not be pleased.

Fortunately, Martin is working with a dedicated theater group, most of them Latino, for the acting studio LAByrinth was initially created for Latino actors. And Guirgis actually used many of the ideas voiced by his actors in his play. The creation of his play (although it's a risky technique) is a collaborative exercise for him. Martin compares an early reading session to what was known in medieval times as a *quodlibetales*. He explains that in the thirteenth century, students at the University of Paris periodically were allowed to engage in an academic "free-for-all." They could toss at their professors any question no matter how wild or absurd.

At the reading sessions, actors were allowed to voice their opinions. They could also make suggestions, were even allowed to compose dialogue. It takes a humble and secure playwright to permit this undertaking, and I must say (though a bit reluctantly) that I admire the spontaneity of the process. It also takes a certain kind of genius to make it all come together and work finally as a play. It will be interesting to see if Guirgis possesses such genius.

On second thought, this process isn't the first time I've heard of it. In the making of what many consider one of Hollywood's finest movies, *Casablanca*, the screenplay wasn't completed at the start of the picture. If I remember correctly, the director didn't know how to end the movie. But look at the results! If I remember correctly, this film always makes the top ten of people's favorite films. Its classic status is definitely secure.

The cast hurls many questions at Father Martin: Who was St. Matthew? Why was his being a tax collector so bad? Did Jesus know he was God? Who was responsible for the death of Jesus? Did Pilate want him dead? Did Caiaphas? What does the "Lamb of God" mean? Why is forgiveness so important in Christian theology? Was Mary Magdalene really married to Jesus, as the *Da Vinci Code* says? How much of Mel Gibson's movie is true?

Answering such deep and challenging questions, Martin was definitely giving his cast a free course in theology! I don't envy his job, because most of these questions are controversial, and by answering them, especially from a Catholic perspective, he would have to step on a few toes. But it's the price of honesty. If you believe in your faith, then you must answer even the most difficult question in the context of what you truly believe. And if you question in a sensitive fashion, I think that rather than annoy or anger people, you will win their respect. Most people, even if they don't agree with you, respect people with convictions.

One of the central concepts of the play is despair. The playwright and the actor playing Judas had to understand despair fully from a theological perspective. Let's face it, even though it's a historical play, it's one that addresses spiritual issues that still apply to modern people. People despair, and like Judas, they sometimes kill themselves.

Thus, the question of culpability must be addressed. Did Judas despair, and if he did, is he not, like all of us, worthy of forgiveness? We enter murky waters with this question. Actually, they aren't so murky from a Catholic perspective. As Martin points out, traditional Catholic theology has maintained that suicide, the result of despair, is a sin, and the punishment is eternal damnation. Today the *Catechism of the Catholic Church* states that some "grave psychological disturbance" can diminish the responsibility of the individual; yet suicide (and despair) is "contrary to love for the living God."

Hamlet's famous "To be or not to be" soliloquy is a meditation on suicide. He's so unhappy and miserable that he'd rather be dead. But possessing a Catholic conscience, he trembles at the thought of the punishment for such an act: hell for eternity. So he chooses "to be" in the hell of his present life rather than go to something far worse. In the same play, there is the scene of Ophelia's burial. She killed herself, but because of her station in the court, strings were pulled, and she was allowed a traditional burial in sacred ground, although some usual rituals were not allowed because of the "suspicion" of suicide.

Even in my youth, I remember a neighbor who had committed suicide, and his family was not allowed to bury their son in the family plot, located in a Catholic cemetery. Today, however, the church isn't as severe in her decisions, taking into consideration the mental state of the person who took his or her life. Should that not be the attitude of a church whose title is Mother Church? What mother would deny her child a proper burial no matter what kind of death? Good question....

Back to Judas. Sam Rockwell *must* know why Judas despaired and *why* he took his life. The answer is pivotal in playing the part. Thus for him, Martin has to answer some pretty difficult questions: Why couldn't God have saved Judas? Was it fair that despair should cause someone to be condemned? Martin's answers, at first, were glib and acceptable, characteristic of many Catholics who believe that some matters are self-evident. A bit of hubris here....

And there were other questions to answer: Doesn't despair derive from a person's psychological makeup. In other words, is it genetic? Ergo, is Judas a victim of predestination? If so, how does the Catholic concept of free will come in? I wouldn't want to have Martin's job!

In one of his serious explanations of despair (the glibness discarded), Martin turned to his favorite modern spiritual writer, Thomas Merton. He quotes Merton: "Despair is the ultimate development of a pride so great and so stiff-necked that it accepts the absolute misery of eternal damnation rather than accept that God is above us and that we are not capable of fulfilling our destinies by ourselves."

Martin is deeply impressed by what Merton said of despair. Merton's reply, however, is traditional Catholicism: the greatest sin is pride, and despair falls under it. Therefore, it is deserving of the worst punishment: damnation.

Such Catholic absolutism, however, didn't convince Guirgis, and he and Martin fall into a debate about free will. Martin, rather than rely on his own intellect and common sense, again quotes another favorite writer, St. Augustine, who argues that we always have free will; therefore, we are free to "choose" despair.

Guirgis challenges Martin's quoting Merton. He just doesn't agree with it. He mentions Jesus' forgiving of Peter. If Peter can be forgiven for denying Christ, why can't Judas be forgiven for betraying him? The reply is that Peter didn't despair, Judas did. The difference between the two men is that one was caught in the abyss of despair, the other wasn't. The engulfing darkness of despair wouldn't allow Judas to perceive Christ's love and mercy. It's a state of soul over which he had no control. A man in despair is blind and often paralyzed.

Furthermore, Merton's quote comes long before he spiritua..., grows as a Catholic. In his early years, as a convert, he was still possessed by the first fervor of faith. Such Catholics don't budge an inch on anything: they are hard on everyone, more so on themselves, as was Merton. If you read his life carefully, you see a man who in the beginning of his life as a monk was being terribly hard on himself. Only later, after much soul-work, does he let up on himself: he learns to love himself and to be more compassionate with himself. In short, he accepts himself: the true road to wisdom.

Martin insists, however, that Judas deserved damnation. He screams into the phone to Guirgis, "You have to participate in your salvation!"

Interesting coincidence, for I often tune into old Mother Angelica shows. She spoke to this very issue of Peter's *betrayal* of Christ, alluding to Christ's warning that he would deny him three times before the cock crowed. But in the Bible Mother Angelica employs, the translation is no longer "betray" but "disowned." Talk about soft-pedaling!

As for the function of free will in our salvation, how often have we Catholics been advised to sacrifice our will to God, as had Christ, "Not my will but Thine be done." Salvation, it seems to me, is more a matter of surrendering; thus, we need not so much participate in our salvation as accept it. It's an idea beautifully captured in George Herbert's poem, "Love."

Love bade me welcome, yet my soul drew back
　　Guilty of dust and sin
But quick-eyed Love, observing me grow slack
　　From my first entrance in,
Drew nearer to me, sweetly questioning,
　　If I lack'd any thing.

"A guest," I answer'd, "worthy to be here";
   Love said, "You shall be he."
"I the unkind, ungrateful? Ah, my dear,
   I cannot look on thee."
Love took my hand, and smiling did reply,
   "Who made the eyes but I?"

"Truth, Lord, but I have marr'd them: let my shame
   Go where it doth deserve."
"And know you not," says Love, "who bore the blame?"
   "My dear, then I will serve."
"You must sit down," says Love, "and taste my meat."
   So I did sit and eat.

After such compassionate encouragement, what guest could fail to sit and eat? But for Judas it was far more complicated. To kill himself is a seeming "No!" to love. But was it indeed a free choice?

As a teacher, I have often dealt with classroom discussions of suicides that occur in several literary works. We discussed the suicides of Ophelia (*Hamlet*), Paul from a story by Willa Cather ("Paul's Case"), the father in Willa Cather's novel *My Antonia*, as well as the suicide of Willie Loman (*Death of a Salesman*).

I don't know why, but young people are fascinated by suicide, and I had to be ever so careful about what I said. Nevertheless, I felt I could not ignore their interest in the subject or their questions about the rightness and wrongness of suicide.

I have to admit, however, I found among my students much more sensitivity and compassion than I found in Christian theology. My students invariably supported the victim of suicide. I say "victim" purposely because they saw that the person who committed suicide was driven to it. As one student quite feelingly wrote (I still have his essay), "When you kill yourself, it's because you're miserable, in hell, and there's no free will left...what person would choose death over life unless he was ill, either psychologically or physically, and in both cases where is the free will?"

His is a good question.

Martin finally admitted to Guirgis that Merton's response to despair, although appealing to Martin himself, was a flawed one. Here I'm a bit surprised that Martin didn't side more quickly with the playwright, for he surely is aware that today we have a deeper understanding of psychology, and that some people are genetically predisposed to depression and suicide. Again, I must keep in mind that the Jesuits formed Martin, and let's face it, formation is a kind of conditioning, and to break free of any kind of conditioning is not easy. In this case, Martin could not safely lean back on what he'd been taught in the seminary. He couldn't just quote an eminent Catholic writer; he had to think for himself, a rather difficult position for a Jesuit priest to find himself in because his purpose is to uphold the teachings of the church. But for matters that have not been decided *ex cathedra*, there is leeway for thinking, for considering matters in a new way.

As a boy, Guirgis was baffled by the notion of a vengeful God, he who previously, up to the third grade, possessed a benign image of God. As a man, he is now challenging the whole idea about a vengeful God, one inculcated in him later. Is not our God one of Love and Mercy? Would God condemn Judas to eternal punishment? It will be interesting to see how much Martin sticks to the party line about Judas being in all likelihood condemned to hell. Being a Jesuit, and therefore a defender of the church, Martin is walking a razor's edge.

If one is intent upon condemning Judas, then it's natural to question the role of Pontius Pilate in his sentence of death for Jesus Christ. Guirgis questions Martin about what Pilate might have thought about being assigned to Judea in the first place. Martin is quick to answer that Pilate would likely have thought Judea to be a backwater, not an important (or cushy) assignment. Guirgis quickly adds this information to his play. It's interesting to me that the playwright is so open to taking and incorporating all that he learns not only from Martin but also from his cast. He is in no sense a directorial diva.

Another example of Guirgis's accepting Martin's suggestions: he incorporates Martin's description of Judea as "armpit of the empire" into his play.

And just when I find myself criticizing Martin for not being open to other ideas, he admits that Judas may indeed deserve the same pity offered to Peter, who denied (betrayed) Christ three times. Yikes! And then seemingly out of nowhere, Martin discusses with Guirgis Mother Teresa, whose private letters and journals had just been published, revealing that she had gone through decades of a "dark night of the soul." She writes that she felt a loss of God, a feeling that God didn't want her, and she even felt at times that God didn't exist. Which taken all together is an accurate description of despair.

Guirgis is moved by Martin's comments about Mother Teresa and instantly felt that he had found the perfect expert witness on despair for his play: Mother Teresa. Genius! And thank you, Father Martin, who opened that particular door for the playwright.

In creating her as a character in his play, Guirgis presents Mother Teresa as hard of hearing, thus needing earphones. Later when discussing the nature of despair, she says that despair is like throwing away one's earphones: "In order to hear, one must be *willing* to listen. When you turn off God, you are saying, 'I know better than you.' No good, boy. No good." (my emphasis)

But again, what if one doesn't have the will to do so?

I like what Martin's and the playwright's discussion led too, for I find the Mother Teresa scene sympathetic. Frankly, it's still in line with traditional Catholic theology so Martin is winning his point with the playwright, who is also Catholic. If I were advising the playwright, I'd suggest, since the play is aimed at all kinds of people with all kinds of beliefs, to aim for ambiguity; the playgoers can leave the theater believing what is convincing and challenging for them.

Again, Mother Teresa's response assumes that the victim of despair still maintains his free will: you must be willing to listen. If you turn off God, she suggests, you do it by will. But the whole point of the discussion is that when a person is in despair, he doesn't see right: he sees nothing but darkness. How can anyone decide where to go if enveloped in crippling darkness?

As I see it, a person in despair is incapable of seeing anything clearly. It's as if he's standing (if he/she has the energy to stand!) in the darkest room possible, without a chink of light, and their eyes, from fear, are closed! Is there anything darker than that?

As for Mother Teresa's metaphor of hearing, well, it's clever, but it doesn't win me over, because I know from experience that when people are gripped by fear, they don't listen to anyone. They can't; fear deafens them. Again (sorry!), where's free will?

Let's get to the nitty-gritty of the play's main theme: Can God forgive a suicide? The answer is yes. Catholics believe in a God of Unconditional Love, Agape. Can God forgive? Yes, because God is a God of infinite love. We human creatures are capable of unconditional love too. Parents, for instance, are capable of forgiving their children of a number of terrible acts and decisions. They can lose everything, robbed by their addict son or daughter, and still love and forgive them. Thus, forgiving Judas falls in the realm of possibility. Of course, agapetic love was not discussed much in the early church. I never heard of it in the twelve years of my Catholic education. I heard plenty about sin and damnation but very little of God's love for us. God was more often presented as a judge not as a lover. Times have finally changed! If we read Dame Julian of Norwich, we are presented with a God who bears no blame toward anyone. And then there is her famous promise from Christ that "all things shall be well."

With the cast of *Judas*, Martin served as more than a theological consultant. He was teacher, advisor, a walking library, lending his books on Christian history and the historical Christ to all the actors in the play. He also became friends with many of the cast as well as their spiritual confidant. Many in the cast were lapsed Catholics, and they felt comfortable discussing their estrangement from the church with Martin, which says a lot about him. Reading between the lines, I know he's an excellent listener. To be a good listener demands humility because it requires that one offer one's full attention to another. In so many of our conversations with other people, including friends and relatives, we often cannot wait, as we half listen, for them to stop so we can have our say. But a good listener puts his own ego on the back burner and really listens to the other, his full attention fixed upon him or her. Attention is one of the greatest gifts we can give to another: it's a form of love. It seems to me that Martin has that wonderful gift: he's attentive to others, he listens. And in the world of the theater, the greatest actors are those who learned the art of listening.

As I said before, I'm a movie buff. I can watch old movies all day on the Turner Classic Movie channel. Robert Osborne, the host, offers insights into the lives of actors. I remember him talking about Spencer Tracy, whom he described as perhaps America's greatest film actor. Tracy was a no-nonsense man when it came to acting. He once chided Katherine Hepburn for hamming it up, if you can imagine anyone telling Hepburn what to do. But she obeyed him. When asked what was the secret of his acting method, Tracy smiled and said it was knowing your lines, saying them, and *looking at* and *listening to* the person to whom you are speaking the lines, and that in good acting, less is more.

Great advice! And not complicated. So many actors today pay good money to join acting studios like Esper, the one most of the actors of *Judas* attended. But I think Tracy's brief advice is the best they could ever receive from an accomplished actor. And just last night the Turner channel ran a brief segment on the career of Hepburn narrated by actor Anthony Hopkins. He made a movie in the 1960s with Hepburn called *The Lion in Winter*. After his first scene with Hepburn, she said to him, "Don't act, just say the lines." In her remark, I could hear the voice of Tracy, with whom Hepburn had been intimate during most of her adult life. She had indeed listened to him and passed on his wisdom.

Martin cleared up a lot of misinformation about Mary Magdalene. Besides Mary the mother of Jesus, there are three Marys in the New Testament (Mary, the woman stoned, Mary of Bethany, and Mary Magdalene), all conflated into one: Mary Magdalene; thus, she is usually identified as Mary the prostitute (the woman to be stoned). According to new biblical scholarship, the woman who washed Christ's feet and dried them with her hair is not Mary Magdalene. The woman about to be stoned for adultery isn't Mary Magdalene. To

41

a lifetime, I was under a gross misconception as to the
Mary Magdalene as were many other Catholics.

the thing is certain: the first person to whom the resurrected
Christ appeared was indeed Mary Magdalene. Why a woman? It's an
issue to which the church should perhaps apply more exegesis in the
future, for its treatment of women, in my opinion, has over the centuries been problematic to say the least.

The books that Martin recommended to the *Judas* cast weren't all
history tomes. He recommended one book on spirituality, one that
helped him greatly when he was a novice working with the poor in
Africa: *Poverty of Spirit* by Johannes Baptist Metz.

Martin felt that the cast shouldn't just concentrate on the visible
personality of the characters they played but also on the spirit that
drove them to become followers of Christ and the kind of spirituality
it demanded. It's a small book but quite dense, and it demands much
pondering. I once owned a copy of the book, and I remember my
impatience with it. In fact, I don't think I finished reading it. Now it's
come back into my life through Martin. I take it as a sign to return to it
and attempt to understand it.

Martin is excellent in emphasizing the book's main points:

1. Poverty of spirit is a radical recognition of our humanity—our
   frail and limited humanity. Many of us cannot bear to confront it.
2. Poverty of spirit does not take away joy. Quite the contrary. It
   is the gateway to joy and happiness...it gives us the freedom to
   say, "It's not all up to me." And when we can say this with
   conviction, we truly become human.
3. Poverty of spirit is also the gateway to gratitude.

4. Poverty of spirit accepts that our reliance on God as the giver of all gifts is a necessary act of humility in the spiritual life.

Such theses are heady stuff for a bunch of world-savvy actors. But the more time Martin spent with the actors, the more he was impressed by their efforts not only to *become* their characters (many of them method actors), but he was also impressed by their attempts to apply what they had learned about their roles to their own lives. One actor, Martin notes, was moved to tears when he saw how many Bibles were to be seen all over the *Judas* set. These actors were taking everything to heart. A lot of this study had to do with the presence of Martin on the set. Surely God was using him for a purpose....

As a Jesuit, Martin was also learning along with the actors. For instance, he hadn't known that the early Jesuits were famous for putting on plays. Between 1650 and 1700, there existed among the five hundred extant schools a "vast international chain of the same number of playhouses, engaged in coordinated production of plays."

It did and didn't surprise Martin. What didn't surprise Martin was that acting in plays would be something to which Jesuits would naturally be attracted. Why? Because St. Ignatius of Loyola's *Spiritual Exercises*, the very book that Thomas Merton studied in order to learn how to meditate while living in his Perry Street apartment in New York City, highly stresses the importance of imagination while meditating, the kind of imagining that Ignatius defines as "composition of place." This means that while meditating on the New Testament stories, one is actually to imagine "being there" with Christ. It's no wonder Jesuits would be attracted to the theater; they consequently became famous for their creative use of scenery and stage props, intricately designed backdrops, and complicated mechanical devices, like trapdoors for ghostly appearances (think of Shakespeare's Globe Theater) and flying machines and apparatuses to simulate clouds.

Martin also learned that Jesuit-staged dramas led to later developments in opera. Jesuits were the forerunners of the cult of opera, for they were the first to encourage music for the masses with musical dramas, cantatas, and oratorios, especially in Germany where it was highly popular.

What *I* didn't know: Molière, Corneille, Racine, and Voltaire were all students of Jesuit schools in France. Extraordinary!

My editor just informed me, when I told him I was now "walking with Martin" in his book *Jesuit Off Broadway*, that this book didn't do as well as Martin's other books. By "do" he meant "sell." I find this hard to believe, for I'm fascinated by it. I think, however, I may know why. In America, interest in plays has fallen off. Americans are either glued to their TVs or attending movies. Actually, Americans are getting used to watching movies through the use of DVDs; thus they can be entertained without stepping out of their living rooms, so the communal aspect of attending movies and plays is being lost in our culture. It's a sad event because we as a country are losing touch with ourselves, and it doesn't bode well for the future.

In particular, attending a play is a rarity for so many of our young people. When I was a teacher, I remember how excited students would become when informed that they as a group would attend a local play, often Shakespeare. Being kids, they first enjoyed the fact that they'd get out of school, but it was always a thrill to listen to students after their seeing a play (for many the first time ever), for they invariably were stimulated by what they saw and heard. Our school had an award-winning drama club, many of the members the fruit of an English curriculum that stressed the importance of reading (and acting out) plays; thus, our students not only studied the classics but modern plays by such writers such as Anton Chekhov, Arthur Miller, Tennessee Williams, and Eugene O'Neill.

There's nothing more exciting than live drama, but it's becoming rarer and rarer in the lives of too many Americans. And it's not just drama but also ballet, opera, and classical music. Pop culture is winning. Kids know rap music by heart but little about Shakespeare, Keats, Shelley, Eliot, Frost, and modern playwrights. Schools in their efforts to be relevant often don't teach what are now considered classics, replacing the latter with books that are on the best-seller's list. It's a loss for each student, and it's a loss for our American culture. Imagine replacing *Oliver Twist* with the *Da Vinci Code*!

Martin entertains all kinds of questions about Jesus Christ from the cast. For him the most intriguing one is: Did Jesus know that he was God? Before he addressed that question, he had to answer another question: How human was Jesus? To answer this query, he turned to his trusted Metz and his *Poverty of the Spirit.* Metz writes,

> Jesus subjected himself to our plight. He immersed himself in our misery and followed our road to the end. He did not escape from the torment of our life....He was not spared from the dark mystery of our poverty as human beings.

There is enough in this brief quotation for a lifetime of meditation, and it certainly answers the question posed.

Back to Jesus' divinity. The Gospel presents a Jesus who is a free man. He is not surprised or disturbed by his arrest in the Garden of

Gethsemane (he already knew he had been betrayed). He even cures the ear of the man Peter attacks, an act that suggests not only Jesus' compassion but that he has also accepted his destiny. Standing before Pilate, he refuses to defend himself. When forced to carry his cross, he does it submissively, embracing/carrying, as it were, his True Self, a life that includes horrific suffering and agonizing death. All of this is evidence of his acceptance of not only the Father's will but his identity: Who He Is.

But again, did he know he was not only human but divine? An important question in this play....

Martin personally believes that Jesus may not have known with certainty that he'd be raised from the dead, the ultimate litmus test for divinity, no question about it. Martin says that he believes Jesus expected something astonishing to happen to him, but did not precisely know what it would be. I don't have the theological background to know whether or not Martin is skating on thin ice with this opinion, but surely he must have checked with others expert in theological matters: he would not wish to be guilty of unorthodoxy!

Not knowing whether Jesus knew about his divinity seemingly isn't a problem for Martin. In fact, his ignorance of his own future makes his ultimate acceptance more meaningful. As for me, it makes him more human, for who among us knows our future, our day and hour of death?

Martin seems to prefer theologian Elizabeth Johnson's idea that upon Jesus' resurrection "his full identity burst upon him with all clarity." Thus, it apparently is this gradual unveiling of the True Self of Jesus that's the most persuasive to Martin.

To be frank, I found Martin is a bit hesitant when dealing with Jesus' knowledge of his divinity. But I admire his willingness as a priest to share his uncertainty, proving that even Jesuits cannot answer all questions. When the church cannot answer a question definitively, she has a stock answer: it's a mystery. While attending Catholic schools for twelve years, I heard that particular expression quite often. The older I become, the more I realize the wisdom of such a comment, because I am indeed in awe of our lives, our world, our cosmos: all such a mystery as well as a miracle.

It's now time for the play's previews. Everyone is anxious, particularly the playwright, who is so pessimistic that he expects his play to be a "train wreck." Even certain lines of the script hadn't yet been ironed out. For instance, when Sam Rockwell, as Judas, refers to the miracle of Cana, he repeats the script's error: "Canaan." Martin can't believe he didn't catch the error before: "It's Cana!" Guirgis yells, covering his face in disbelief. And this mistake just before the previews!

The other problem is that no one actually knows how long the play will last. Is it a two-hour play or a three-hour play? To me this sounds incredulous, but Guirgis wrote the play as it unfolded before his (and the cast's) very eyes. It's the way he works. I don't think it's the best way to create a play, as I said before, but it's his way of doing it. It's terribly risky, nevertheless.

Then at the last moment, Guirgis writes new dialogue for Jesus, which undercuts the personality of Jesus created before these new words. Martin vehemently expressed his surprise and convinced the playwright that the new dialogue just wouldn't work. To his credit, Guirgis listened to Martin, followed his advice, and composed a more compelling exchange between Judas and Jesus.

Again, it comes down to attentively listening, not only in the theater world but in life, one on one.

47

As the previews continued, Martin observed in amazement how the play continued to improve, the amusing scenes funnier, the sad scenes sadder, the play becoming tighter and tighter. But, of course, with every theatrical production, everyone is anxious about opening night. The word *anxious* actually doesn't capture what the cast, playwright, and director must feel. It surely is something closer to terror, or at least that's how I think I'd feel: terrified!

Opening night arrives. Lots of the cast's friends and family were there, but there were also present important people from the New York acting community, actors as eminent as Meryl Streep. The play received mixed reviews. New York reviews tended to be bad, missing the whole point of the play, but the critic from the *Guardian* of London wrote that it was an "extraordinary" play. The *New Republic* said the play "confirms Guirgis's place as one of our most electric young dramatists"; *Time Out New York* wrote that it was a "must-see" for the week. *Commonweal* said the play was a "landmark event in contemporary American theater"; *Entertainment Weekly* called it "unjustly overlooked." A mixed bag indeed....

To be candid, I feel that to write an essentially Christian play is a daring act in our secular society, especially to have it premiered in a city like liberal New York; liberals, when they imagine Christians, usually see far-right Evangelicals. Sophisticated theater aficionados would likely not attend a play addressing such an overtly Christian theme; its very title would turn them off. Too bad. From what I've read of the play, through Martin's eyes of course, it's a challenging play, one that moves people, gets them thinking, and even inspires them.

When you leave any play and find yourself still thinking about it, then in my book, it's a success. Martin believes that's what happened to those who attended the play; they left it thinking. There was, how-ever, one valid criticism: the play was two hours and forty-five min-utes long. Just too long for today's audience. Remember, our age is that of ADD, not only for kids, but for adults!

Martin made many good friends during his time with *Judas*; conse-quently, he felt sad about leaving them. To mark the ending of his exciting experience, he offered Mass at St. Ignatius Loyola Church, and to his delight, a lot of the cast showed up. As one cast member said, "You came to see *our* show....How could we miss yours?" The Mass as show? Well, in a sense it is: a priest can celebrate Mass beau-tifully—or not. I've seen Mass celebrated so beautifully that it brings tears to my eyes, but there have been Masses celebrated so quickly and seemingly without reverence that I've left the church sad and sorely disappointed. Many Catholics have experienced the same....

Martin is, of course, saddened by the poor reception and the short run of the play. All those hours of creation, of rehearsing, of physical and mental labor, all for naught. Well, not for naught, for the cast will always have the memory of performing in a rather special play. Because they are professionals, the actors early on learn to deal with rejection and failure. To be an actor, one must be passionate about act-ing. It means living without security, to be plagued by the question, "When will I next be offered a job?" It's not a lifestyle I'd choose for myself. I like to know I'll receive a weekly paycheck and be able to pay my rent and bills. It's why so many actors are forced to take on poorly paying jobs, like the perennial job of waiters in restaurants (New York City has plenty of them!), and forced to live a gypsy kind of life, often depending on friends and family when times are tough, by which I mean a time of no acting roles.

During the run of the play, Guirgis allowed after the play what's described as "talk-backs." Audience members are encouraged to remain after the play to question the actors about the play. It's an ordeal for actors to engage in such an exercise because acting itself is exhausting, but everyone in the cast was willing to answer questions if they helped to shed light on the purpose of the play. Guirgis himself concisely answered why he wrote the play to begin with: "I never write with a result in mind....But I hoped the play would cause nonreligious people to reconsider things, religious people to think about how strong their faith is, and those in between to be stimulated to embrace spirituality, a bit. And that seems to have happened, and that's meant a lot to me."

All artists console themselves with the belief that when one person is moved by their art, then it was all worth it. Guirgis admits to receiving more e-mail about this play than anything else he had written. It must have been uplifting for him, considering that most people described his play as "unsuccessful."

My final word about the play comes through Sam Rockwell. He said, "I guess I know more about Jesus and his message. But I just hope I don't fake it or take it for granted now, because during these last few months there was this feeling in me, this feeling that I had just a little more faith."

My final word on this book: it should be read by every aspiring actor. Martin penetrated the masks of his actors, no easy task for they are well trained to assume masks. He learned about what makes an actor, and he was able to do so because the cast members were comfortable enough with him to *be themselves*, to share their inner lives with him. That says a lot about Martin the man and Martin the priest.

V

I've just finished reading Martin's memoir, *My Life with the Saints*, for which he received the Christopher Award as well as the Catholic Press Association Book Award. In it, he devotes chapters to the saints who become his "companions" in life. These "saints" (some haven't been officially canonized) are people he admires and tries to emulate.

I remember once reading a comment by the eminent literary critic Harold Bloom saying that poets helped him to live his life. It's high praise from a man of extraordinary intellectual brilliance. Martin could have easily said, "Saints help me to live my life." Although he doesn't actually come out and overtly say these words, he actually believes it. Thus, each chapter in his memoir is devoted to one of the "saints" he has found along his way through life. And I use the word *found* in the fullest sense of its meaning, for Martin comes across some of his saints accidentally (are there such things as "accidents"?). Some of them he knows almost nothing about, but once "touched" by a saint, he makes it his business to learn as much as he can about her/him.

Like any good Jesuit (invariably cerebral!), Martin starts his memoir with a definition of terms. What is a saint? For help he turns to Lawrence S. Cunningham's *The Meaning of Saints*. Cunningham has a useful description for saints; they are "prophetic witnesses" who spur us to live more fully as Christians. Martin mentions that to be more Christ-like, simply emulate Jesus. True. On the other hand, if

God provides us saints to accompany us along the way, to inspire us, why not accept their example?

We all need exemplars of human holiness before us because they encourage us; they prove to us that holiness is a real possibility for us all. We also have the added advantage of being able to pray to saints (those canonized). They can intervene with God for us. Furthermore, it's a secure feeling to know that we have the saints on our side; they want for us what is good for us. Martin understands this aspect of sainthood, and for different needs, he turns to different saints.

It is an act of humility to pray to saints. Every time we pray to a saint, we admit that we need help, that we can't be the kind of Christian we want to be without supernatural help.

The first saint Martin venerated as a youngster was St. Jude. He had purchased an inexpensive statue of the Saint of the Impossible and kept it atop his bedroom bureau. He didn't know much about St. Jude, but it was consoling to have the statue stand on the bureau watching over him. However, if he ever had friends over, the statue was immediately dispatched into the sock drawer! Little things, like an inexpensive statue, can later play an important role in our lives. With Martin, he "collected" an array of saints, canonized and uncanonized, whom he made his companions.

The first saint about whom he writes at length is St. Joan of Arc. St. Joan is famous for saving the city of Orleans from the English in 1429. For that victory, she has been called the "Maid of Orleans." She is famous also for hearing voices, primarily that of St. Catherine of Alexandria, but there were also others. For a time she was France's hero. Later she ran afoul of certain powerful church leaders. Joan had alienated many of them because of her insistence that she heard heavenly voices and her insistence on wearing soldier's garb. She was later railroaded in a church court where she was denounced as a heretic.

How ironic: denounced by the church and later canonized! An all-too-familiar story in church history, one I find disturbing, quite frankly. When she was burned at the stake (!), it is reported that her last words were "Jesus, Jesus." To explain these shameful events in our church history, my teachers always would say that our church was composed of imperfect men and women; therefore, our church cannot be perfect. It's an argument I never fully bought into, and still don't.

Martin is a movie buff. He wanted to learn about St. Joan and found several films about her to be helpful in understanding her personality. Indeed, there are several fine films about her: one with Ingrid Bergman as St. Joan and another with Jean Seberg. Martin also made a trip to Orleans, France. As a student he had chosen to study French, so visiting France was a good test of how much French he had learned in school.

What astonishes Martin about St. Joan are the illogical aspects of her story (again the cerebral Jesuit!). She was a peasant girl who couldn't read or write. She couldn't even sign her forced confession and simply made a sign of the cross. She had had access to the dauphin of France and to church leaders and led the French army against the English, but because she insisted that she talked to saints, she was excommunicated from the church.

Illogical? Yes, to say the least.

Martin's introduction to the Little Flower, St. Thérèse of Lisieux, was actually accomplished through a movie, *Thérèse*. I know the movie well, and I remember the controversy it caused among Catholics because at the end of her life, she was caught in a dark night of the soul. She seemingly died in darkness, not what we Catholics would call a happy death (other than dying in a state of grace), for which many of us pray every time we pray the Hail Mary : "...pray for us now and at the hour of our death." The movie is a stark portrayal of her life, not an easy one to say the least. And her death was a horrifically painful one.

On the way out of the movie theater, Martin's friend remarked, "What a waste of a life." This comment shocked Martin, and he profusely defended the saint, simultaneously commenting on suffering, the value of sacrifice, the role of faith and love. He was touched by her life and was glad to have viewed the movie. The surprising thing is that as a Catholic he previously knew nothing about her.

He later notes that one of the best ways to be introduced to a saint is through a movie. To support his opinion, he cites Robert Bolt's play *A Man for All Seasons* about the life of Sir Thomas More, brilliantly acted by Paul Scofield. He won the Tony Award for his performance of Sir Thomas More on Broadway. Later, he won the Oscar for the film version. As a young man I saw it and was mesmerized by his performance.

I must admit, however, when I later learned that More had ordered men and women put to death for supposed heresy, I wasn't so much a fan of the man—or the saint. But it's only my opinion, and I'm certain a reply to my disturbance would again be that we are all imperfect creatures in an imperfect world. How can one argue against that? To the church's credit, she is finally admitting to her past mistakes (for example, Galileo, her treatment of Jews)—always a good step in the right direction.

But seeing a movie isn't sufficient for historical accuracy. Martin also reads biographies and autobiographies. He reads Thérèse's autobiography *The Story of a Soul*. He ends up admiring this young woman who at fifteen seeks dispensation from the pope to allow her to enter a Carmelite convent before she turns sixteen. At first, the pope refuses her request, but with dogged insistence, she maintained her campaign, and her local bishop finally granted her permission.

The Little Flower (as St. Thérèse is famously known) was in fact no delicate flower. Martin observes that she was a tough, determined person who had what her biographer Kathryn Harrison calls "a genius of secret mortification." The young woman offered her small, daily hardships to Christ, for she felt she was incapable of heroic actions. Thus, she'd offer up to God the small annoyances caused by nuns who teased her or who were deliberately unkind to her. The unkindest nuns were the ones she tried to love the most. Her method of spirituality was later described as her "Little Way." Although she was not learned, the church, after canonizing her only twenty-eight years after her death, later made her a doctor of the church along with two other women, St. Catherine of Siena and St. Teresa of Avila.

Martin may see himself, I believe, in St. Thérèse. His way to sainthood will unlikely become the way of martyrdom (although one never knows!) or intense persecution but more likely by following a "Little Way." I think this is true for most of us. About ten or eleven years ago I was in New York City—my memory isn't as accurate as it used to be so I'm not sure if it was St. Patrick's Cathedral or not—and I saw a crowd of people entering a church. On asking, I was told that relics of St. Thérèse of Lisieux were on display. I remember thinking how amazing it was that so many people living in New York City, which many call Sin City, would turn out to go to see a saint's relics. New York City relishes its reputation for sophistication, for being the world's center of fashion and art. But a little saint from France, a dead saint, was attracting large crowds in Manhattan. Amazing!

Martin considers Thomas Merton a saint. Let's face this issue of sainthood head-on. What is the chance of Merton's ever being canonized? Small. Even though he was one of the most important voices of American Catholicism in the twentieth century and remains one in the twenty-first century, I see no group in the church advocating for his sainthood, as immediately happened with Mother Teresa and Pope John Paul II. Why? His dissolute youth, his supposed fathering of a child out of wedlock, and his romance with a nurse when he was a monk will likely end any attempt to begin a movement toward presenting his name for sainthood.

Is this fair? Of course not, but it's the way it is. I'm always amazed that St. Augustine was canonized. If anyone lived a profligate life before his conversion, it was Augustine. He also fathered a child out of wedlock. But the way saints are canonized today renders it virtually impossible for so very humanly flawed but holy people like Dorothy Day (more of her later) and Merton to become saints of our church. If their flaws are related to sexuality—well, it's all over! It's why Henri Nouwen will also never be considered for canonization: his ambivalent sexual nature will shut the door. But by all accounts, he was indeed a saintly man, faithful to his vows.

So it's a bit daring for Martin to refer to Merton as a saint, but I say, good for him!

I won't go into much detail about Martin's companionship with Merton, having already addressed it. But Martin is insightfully astute at summarizing what drew Merton into the church in the first place: the Catholic Church appealed to his intellect, to his aesthetic appreciation, and to his emotions.

Intellectually: Gilson's *The Spirit of Medieval Philosophy* challenged him. Aesthetically: The beauty of frescoes of Christ in Rome's great churches moved him as he gazed upon them for hours. Emotionally: Watching his father die of brain cancer caused him to question the meaning of life in general and his own life specifically. Intellect, aesthetics, emotions: all three worked on Merton, Martin says. Thus his conversion wasn't an immediate but a gradual one, though when he had first read Merton's autobiography he misread it, thinking that Merton's conversion fell under the category of a big-bang event, similar to a Billy Graham conversion, swiftly embracing Jesus as one's Lord and Savior. Not the case with Merton. Lots of thought, prayer, reading, and time preceded his baptism at Corpus Christi Church near Columbia University.

When Merton first sees the Abbey of Gethsemani, he is overwhelmed by it, feeling that he had finally found his true home. Martin says that after reading Merton's autobiography, he felt, "I had come home." He writes, "For me, Thomas Merton's description of religious life was an invitation to a new life."

Merton's book exerted a similar effect on the post-World War II generation of men (many of them former soldiers). Because of Merton's autobiography, Gethsemani was flooded with requests for admission. There were so many candidates at the abbey that they didn't have enough room to house them, and many of them had to sleep in the corridors. Merton's book caused a rebirth at Gethsemani (royalties from his book[s] put the abbey back on its feet financially) as well as increased interest in other Catholic monasteries in America. Before long, with each of his books a best seller, he became the voice of American Catholicism. No other Catholic, except Fulton Sheen, could challenge his popularity among Catholic readership.

Martin's favorite prayer is also mine. I have the prayer card in front of me now. I must write it out because there are likely readers unfamiliar with it. It can be prayed by any Christian, not just Catholics:

My Lord God, I have no idea where I am going. I do not see the road ahead of me. I cannot know for certain where it will end. Nor do I really know myself, and the fact that I think I am following your will does not mean that I am actually doing so. But I believe that the desire to please you does in fact please you. And I hope I have that desire in all that I am doing. I hope that I will never do anything apart from that desire. And I know that if I do this you will lead me by the right road, though I may know nothing about it. Therefore I will trust you always though I may seem to be lost and in the shadow of death. I will not fear, for you are ever with me, and you will never leave me to face my perils alone. (Thomas Merton, *Thoughts in Solitude*)

It's a beautiful prayer, and Merton aficionados everywhere know it by heart.

When Martin becomes interested in one of his saintly companions, he is intent upon learning more about them. With Joan of Arc, he made many visits to Orleans; with St. Thérèse; he not only saw every film about her but also read many books about her, including her autobiography. With Merton, not only did he read his books (he has a particular fondness for Merton's *The Sign of Jonas*, which was actually my favorite Merton book when I was young), he also visited the Abbey of Gethsemani in Kentucky. His first reaction was the same as mine when I went there: it was an extremely hot place to live and at first sight rather harsh looking, quite different from the beautiful landscape of St. Joseph's Abbey here in Massachusetts. I had gone to Gethsemani in August and could hardly breathe the heat-scorched air. How the monks could bear to wear their heavy habits in such hot weather was a mystery to me, and surely a penance for them.

At the end of the chapter on Merton, Martin, standing at Merton's grave, imagines what he would say to Merton, "I thought of every-thing I would like to say to Thomas Merton: That there was probably no other person other than Jesus so responsible for my vocation."

It's a stunning admission. He perhaps has the right to think of Merton as a saint. I myself think he's likely a saint, already enjoying the Beatific Vision. But I don't believe the church will ever canonize him. It's too bad because in his flawed, human way, he had much more in common with everyday men and women than many of those now included in our pantheon of saints.

Merton liked booze, was sexy, was funny, but he also loved God, prayed every day of his life at Gethsemani, and through his writings led many people to God and religious vocations. But it's just not good enough for canonized sainthood. What's amusing is that Merton wouldn't have cared a bit about being declared a saint. He learned in the monastery that to be a saint means being *yourself*.

Martin keeps that piece of wisdom always before him, as if there is an inner voice constantly whispering: I have to be myself.

Being a Jesuit, Martin must include as one of his companions St. Ignatius of Loyola. Here I have to admit a bias: I don't like Ignatius of Loyola, never have. My dislike began with my reading of his *Spiritual Exercises*, a book that I dislike because of its too heavy emphasis on sin and guilt; its commentaries on hell are downright scary. No wonder James Joyce turned against his church. His hell and brimstone sermon in *Portrait of the Artist as a Young Man* is right out of Ignatius's *Spiritual Exercises*. Frankly, I've had enough Catholic homilies on hell, sin, and guilt to last a lifetime. Furthermore, such homilies have driven from the church too many of my relatives and friends. How rarely we heard about God's unconditional love for us. It's called *agape* (Greek). I never in twelve years of Catholic education heard the word *agape* uttered in any of my classes or in any homily in my parish.

Before addressing the life of Ignatius, Martin describes his own life as a Jesuit novice. He had to spend fifteen hours of ministry outside the novitiate, working at a local Catholic hospital. He had to cook once a week for the other novices, to attend daily Mass, to pray at least an hour a day, to participate in weekly spiritual direction and faith-sharing meetings at night before bed.

There was also a daily hour-long conference held at 8:00 a.m. His was a busy life to say the least. And, of course, they had to learn about the founder of their religious order, Ignatius of Loyola. Thus, he had to read a number of books by and about the saint.

He mentions one astonishing fact: Ignatius penned 6,813 letters! Yikes!

Martin offers a brief biography of Ignatius, but the most important event occurred when the soldier/dandy's leg was hit by a cannon-ball. He nearly lost his leg and had a limp for the rest of his life. It was while recuperating after an operation that Ignatius began to consider the direction of his life. He didn't like where it seemed to be heading: a life similar to the young Augustine's.

Illness is sometimes a good thing. It slows people down, allowing them to take an inward look at themselves. It happened to Ignatius, and when he began to read the lives of the saints, he knew he had to change his lifestyle. He assumed the life of a poor pilgrim and made the usual visit to Jerusalem. His piety impressed other young men and, before long, he had six faithful followers. They decided to call themselves *Societas Jesu* in Latin, the Company of Jesus, whose purpose was the "helping of souls."

Soon after, the pope approved his order, centered in Rome. At the very heart of Ignatius's constitution is a fervent dedication to the pope. Thus, the order has always had a close affiliation with the supreme leader of the Catholic Church. What I didn't know is that in the beginning Ignatius's men were called "Jesuits" *derisively*, a word of insult crafted by Ignatius's critics.

Under the influence of religion, Ignatius became a severe, austere man. The life he devised for those who joined him was a challengingly rigorous one. Martin quotes a fellow Jesuit's comment on his afterlife judgment: "I have no problem with Jesus judging me. It's Ignatius I'm worried about!"

Ah! Martin says exactly what I caught onto years ago: "The *Spiritual Exercises* is not a compendium of warm reflections on the love of God." I've got to hand it to him, Martin is honest, even about the founder of his order. Again, good for him!

Martin is fair, however. He writes:

Ignatius found God everywhere: in the poor, in prayer, in the Mass. In his fellow Jesuits, in his work, and, most touchingly, on the balcony of the Jesuit house in Rome, where he loved to gaze up silently at the stars at night. During these times he would shed tears in wonder and adoration. His emotional responses to the presence of God in his life gives the lie to the stereotype of the cold saint.

But in the end, Martin cannot escape his True Self and admits that Ignatius is indeed a distant figure, severe and demanding. But he includes him as one of his favorite companions, comparing him to a harsh relative who, although a pain in the neck, was the uncle or aunt who secretly provided the funds for one's education.

What I didn't particularly like about Ignatius's *Spiritual Exercises* is its emphasis on *examination of conscience*. All Jesuits practice it (or rather they are supposed to). It's a final review of one's day to discover if you've been a good, faithful follower of Christ (and, of course, of Ignatius). But it's a practice that I believe can lead to a crippling scrupulosity as it did with another famous Jesuit, Gerard Manley Hopkins. At the end of a grueling day—and most priests have busy, crowded lives—to have to recall all of one's faults, sins, and failures of the day, well, it seems to me counterproductive. Why not a simple act of contrition, skip the blow-by-blow "sins" of the day and have a good night's sleep?

The more Martin writes about Ignatius, the more his ambivalence about him is evident. He admits that he doesn't have the same affection for Ignatius as he has for Thérèse of Lisieux or Thomas Merton and can't see himself lingering over passages of Ignatius's writing the way he muses upon passages from *The Story of a Soul* and *The Seven Storey Mountain*. Martin finally confesses that he just can't get close to Ignatius. To me it's understandable, but I also know there are many Catholics who are indeed fond of Ignatius. Well, as I always say, each to his own.

VI

I've spent the last few months finishing (or rather rewriting) my book *Walking with Gerard Manley Hopkins.* Even though I had to suspend my reading of Martin, I seemingly encountered him everywhere: NPR, TV, *America* (of which he's the cultural editor), and YouTube. Friends, knowing I'm writing a book on Martin, often phone or e-mail me of Martin sightings. He seems to be ubiquitous!

Much of his seeming omnipresence has to do with his new book *The Jesuit Guide to (Almost) Everything: A Spirituality for Real Life,* published by HarperOne. Just recently, I opened my *America* to find a large two-page advertisement of his new book. My first thought (as an author) was how fortunate for Martin to have his publisher pay for such a fine, alluring ad since, in all my publishing history, I'd never had any of my publishers do much (if any!) advertising of my books. In short, I was envious.

Then the following month Martin received an excellent review of his book in *America,* one written by Sister Janice Farnham. Simply to say it was a glowing review is understatement. Her comments convinced me that the next Martin book I should read is this one, already on the *New York Times* best-seller's list. Yes, Father Martin has hit the big time with this book. It has widened his audience, which was already a large and faithful one. Now he's becoming a household name. So today I begin his *Jesuit Guide.*

I suspect I'll not feel too uncomfortable with *The Jesuit Guide.* As I mentioned, I served Mass for Jesuit priests from grades six to eight. I looked up to these priests to such a degree that I'd entertained the idea of becoming a Jesuit. But in high school I was assigned to read Thomas Merton's autobiography, and the Trappists quickly became my ideal religious order. In the end, however, I concluded priesthood was not my vocation, a surprise for my family, my teachers, and my priest counselor/confessor.

Before I delve into Martin's book, I think I'll jot down some more of my own impressions of Jesuits. For the most part, I found them aloof. Many of them were academics teaching either at Boston College High School or at Boston College. They didn't banter with us altar boys. We served their Mass, and to them it was our only purpose. Their sermons were usually focused on the day's Gospel, and some were long-winded, others mercifully brief. As for celebrating Mass, I remember how some of them seemed to become lost in the Mass. They, at least to my youthful imagination, had entered another dimension. There was one unforgettable Jesuit who celebrated Mass in slow motion. A low Mass could take up to fifty minutes (no homily included). I remember seeing people walk into church, and when Father X exited the sacristy, they would quickly rush out of the church!

I sometimes worked in the rectory office; it had to be manned well into the evening. It was only then did I achieve a different insight into the lives of these priests. At the beginning of the stairs to the third floor a sign proclaimed "Cloister." I'd often been upstairs to serve priests in their private chapel. I was always thrilled to enter this other, unknown, world, offering me an inside peek at their way of life. I saw nothing outstanding. Their bedrooms were like everyone else's: some bedrooms a mess of unmade beds, books strewn everywhere and desks piled high with papers, others neat and orderly as if cleaned by a maid. The common room was inviting with large comfortable chairs.

Before dinnertime, while sitting at the office desk, I'd often hear laughter coming from upstairs. And I'd smile, thinking that there was another side to these men who for the most part kept to themselves and rarely let down their guard. Little did I know at the time that Jesuits have a common practice of having drinks before dinner; it would come under the title of *preprandium*. So alcohol loosened them up. Good for them, I thought when I later found out it was indeed their cocktail time.

I remember when I studied at Fordham, I was invited, along with the other members of the fellowship, to dine with the Jesuits. We first, however, had cocktails. I remember meeting Father Avery Dulles. When I was introduced to him, I went to shake his hand, but one hand held a book while the other held what looked like a Scotch and soda. He immediately solved the problem by extending his pinky finger. Which I shook! I still laugh at this absurd gesture of greeting, for this man would later become a cardinal of the church!

I mention these observations now because I don't have Jesuits placed too high on a pedestal. I've had a glimpse of their humanity. And I'm not in awe of them. This perspective is a good one to have as I more deeply enter Martin's Jesuit world. I recall that when I first began writing the first of five books about Thomas Merton, I had placed him on a very high pedestal so very beyond us ordinary people. Thus, much of my writing about him had been mere hero-worshiping. I was finally able to gain a more reasonable perspective and to write about him more objectively. As for Martin, as I mentioned, I don't know him very well anyway so there's no danger of subjectivity. I simply want to learn more about him, and I want to be fair in my estimation of him as a person and as a priest. I hope that when I come to the end of reading him, I *like* the man. So far, I do. But only time will tell....

Resolution: to make a journal entry every day. If I do one faithfully, I can finish this book by Christmas (it didn't happen!). And I can then resume writing my novel. I'm more and more drawn to writing fiction.

Read a good portion of Martin's book last night. He instantly informs his readers that they will have to learn about Ignatian spirituality because it's the bedrock of Jesuit life. He seemingly has completely adopted the Ignatian way of life and advises his readers that it's a good way to live. He lists the most important of life's questions, ones he believes Ignatius answers wisely.

How do I know what I'm supposed to do in life?
How do I know who I'm supposed to be?
How do I make good decisions?
How can I be a good friend?
How can I face suffering?
How can I be happy?
How can I find God?
How do I pray?
How do I love?

These are surely the basic questions most of us have about life. But I would reduce all these questions to one: How can I be a good Christian? This simple question encompasses the nine questions above. He explains that Ignatius would encourage people to become contemplatives-in-action. His way of life is not a passive but an active one (it's paradoxical: we are to be contemplative and active, not an easy way of life). We are to see ourselves as men and women who live in the world, but we should view the world as a monastery. Not a new concept; others have employed this analogy, but it's one I find intriguing.

I myself, although not a monk, consider my life rather monastic, for my secular life as a layperson also revolves around the monastic ideal of Ora et Labora, Prayer and Work.

Martin summarizes his chapter on Ignatian spirituality by listing its hallmarks:

Finding God in all things
Becoming a contemplative in action
Looking at the world in an incarnational way
Seeking freedom and detachment

It becomes quite clear as one reads Martin's book that he has embraced without question the Jesuit way of life. I am always a little uneasy with such a perspective, as if one person (Ignatius) could have all the answers to life's questions. I myself tend to be more eclectic, taking wisdom from many sources and traditions to help me lead my life: to rely on only one person's insights, well, it's a bit risky if not dangerous, and in a worst-case scenario, it can lead to fanaticism.

For instance, Ignatius's conversion had much to do with his reading the lives of the saints while he was convalescing. Then he decided, well, I will be a saint too. That literally was his decision. My problem with such a decision is that there's too much ego involved. God makes saints, no individual does. Merton made the same mistake. Because his friend Robert Lax said being a saint should now be Merton's purpose in life (Merton had just converted to Catholicism), Merton embraced the idea literally, thus causing himself much heartache and disappointment. To decide to become a saint is quite a burden to assume. The better way is simply to surrender oneself to God, and pray, "Do with me what you will," and leave saint making to God.

Of course, some would argue, what would you expect of such a decision from a Jesuit: they are masters at conditioning their priests. I remember hearing someone repeating the idea of Jesuits' promising parents that if they gave their children to Jesuit education, they would forever belong to the church. It's quite true that Jesuits, over the centuries, have won for their order a reputation as one of the world's greatest group of educators.

So is Martin simply a well-conditioned Jesuit and has he simply bought "into" the Jesuit way of life hook, line, and sinker? On one level, I would have to say that he has. But it's not a question of any kind of against-the-will, inflicted-force, or unfair conditioning process. He embraced Jesuit life when he was an adult after he had experienced the world. It satisfied his needs, and it's all that matters.

We all eventually embrace a way of life. We may not define or name it, but in essence, we have chosen a way of life; otherwise, we probably couldn't get out of bed in the morning. Once we rise in the morning, we affirm that life is worth living. Then, likely without our intellectualizing it, we set into motion our "way" of living. We perform certain habitual actions, and they somehow get us through the day. It's our "system" although, again, we may never have actually thought it through: we just do it, that is, we live.

Martin, to borrow from Wallace Stevens, has found the Jesuit way of life to be "sufficient." Actually, he finds it more than sufficient because the purpose of his book is to convince his readers that they could become happier people if they too embraced the Ignatian way of life. At this point, I'm quite intrigued about how he'll go about presenting his case.

Well, I have to admit that Martin is forthright. On page 26, he announces quite emphatically the purpose of his book:

This book is an introduction to the way of St. Ignatius Loyola, at least as I've learned it in my twenty-one years as a Jesuit. It's not meant to be overtly scholarly or academic. Instead, it's a friendly introduction for the general reader.

His sentence reminds me of the question all my publishers have always asked me of my books: "What audience of readers do you intend to reach?" surely an important question for marketing purposes. I, like Martin, have always aimed my books at the general reader. I consider myself a general reader, although I'm eclectic in my choice of books: I read all kinds of books, including those that Martin refers to as "academic." Many general readers are open to various genres and subjects. Martin's book will appeal to people interested in developing their spiritual lives, but I'm sure there are many readers who just want to learn more about Jesuits. The Society of Jesus has a mystique that has intrigued generations of Catholics (and non-Catholics); thus, I believe his book will likely sell well (in fact, it already is a best seller!).

While I'm on the subject of Jesuits, I am reminded of two spiritual icons who were very attracted to the Jesuits. One is Gerard Manley Hopkins. After graduating with a First from Oxford University, Hopkins had decided he possessed a religious vocation. He narrowed the choice of religious orders down to two: the Benedictines and the Jesuits. True to form, Hopkins chose the Jesuits because they were well known for the rigor of their training. Hopkins never took the easy way. He was also attracted to the Jesuit's emphasis on education: most Jesuits go on to higher education, many of them becoming scholars in a number of fields, not just theology and philosophy (more later).

The other icon is Thomas Merton. He wasn't in any way attracted to the Jesuit order. He had narrowed his two choices to the Franciscans and the Trappists. Like Hopkins (about whom Merton had hoped to write his dissertation), he too chose the more rigorous of the two religious orders. But he was, as mentioned, briefly attracted to St. Ignatius's *Spiritual Exercises*. Once he chose to become a Trappist, he seemed to lose all interest in St. Ignatius. His favorite mystic became St. John of the Cross, later to be replaced by Dame Julian of Norwich, author of *The Revelations of Divine Love*.

I believe Merton found both St. Ignatius and St. John of the Cross too strict, too rigorous in their spiritual disciplines, in short, too ascetical, too obsessed with sin and with too little emphasis on God's love and mercy. This opinion is quite simply my own; thus, it doesn't make it true. But I do find it interesting to note that during my intense study of Merton's work over the last few years (culminating in my last book on Merton, *The Wounded Heart of Thomas Merton*), that both Ignatius and John of the Cross seem to disappear from the screen of Merton's mind, whereas Lady Julian looms larger and larger as Merton grew older (in my opinion, as he grew wiser!). Frankly, I believe I know why (again, this is simply my opinion): Lady Julian of Norwich is so brimful of love, compassion, and humanity. Rather than emphasizing God's wrath over man's sin, she invariably speaks of God's unwavering, unconditional love of each one of us. And, of course, there's her famous promise from Christ, "All manner of things shall be well," the very words that saved T. S. Eliot from despair. I also believe this very promise uplifted Merton (he read carefully Eliot's *Four Quartets*, whose last quartet addresses Lady Julian and Christ's promise), who was plagued by guilt for a good portion of his adult life: Merton needed Julian in his life, and he has written about her with great love and admiration.

As for myself, I once as a young man tried to embrace the *Spiritual Exercises*, but they did nothing for me. I really can't explain why. I do remember distrusting their emphasis on the imagination. I'd rather not turn my spiritual life over to my imagination. The sine qua non of my inner life is the Mass and the Gospels. As for imagining the Gospels by Ignatius's method of "composition of place," well, I'd rather read the Gospels as they are and let Matthew, Mark, Luke, and John simply relate their narrative. Perhaps this view is cut-and-dried, but the Gospels don't need the purple prose of my rather active, healthy imagination.

It will be interesting to read Martin's response to the *Spiritual Exercises*. If he's enthusiastic about them, I'll, of course, wonder why. It will be interesting to see *how* he'll convince modern readers to turn to Ignatius's methodology because in the last few decades I've noticed that people have more and more turned to such mystics as Teresa of Avila, Hildegarde von Bingen, and Lady Julian (all women). Of course, St. Francis of Assisi is always popular, but Ignatius has not been a part of that illustrious, attractive group of "modern" spiritual mentors that today's readership seems to prefer. Even the difficult Meister Eckhart is more popular than Ignatius.

Martin lists six Paths of Faith:

The Path of Belief
The Path of Independence
The Path of Disbelief
The Path of Return
The Path of Exploration
The Path of Confusion

He clearly defines each path even though there are contradictions that he too facilely glides over. About The Path of Belief, he makes the sweeping statement: "Ultimately, faith is a gift from God." Well, if that's the case, then a person truly can't do anything to win faith; thus, it seemingly nullifies all the other ways he has listed. But he then qualifies his commentary by saying that a person's soul is like a garden that must be cultivated and nourished. Thus, if you are true to your cultivation and gardening habits, faith will indeed bloom. Therefore, it's not so much a gift as it is the fruit of—soul-work and prayer?

I know many people who are agnostics and atheists: they long to believe in God and the immortality of the soul, but wanting faith doesn't mean you will achieve it. Perhaps Martin is more accurate to simply support his first comment: faith is a gift from God. But then the next question, for me anyway, is why does God gift some people with faith and deny others? A conundrum to say the least!

The Path of Independence addresses people who do not embrace any religion. They are eclectic when it comes to joining churches; some do, others don't. Martin believes that their main defect is their perfectionism: they expect people (churches that is) to be perfect and when they meet so much imperfection (and they will), they flee in a panic. Well, I sympathize with such people because the "faithful" are often the worst advertisements for churches. You would expect people who "practice" their Christian religion to be kind, tolerant, compassionate, and forgiving. But so often we find so little of such virtues within our churches (I refer to the laity as well as the professed). Again, we can fall on the old, classic argument (here it is again!) that you can't expect a church to be perfect when it's composed of imperfect human beings. A neat argument, but it's, as I've already said, not a convincing one. Martin sees perfectionism as a stumbling block to God; however, did not Christ say, "Be ye perfect as your heavenly Father is perfect"?

Playing devil's advocate with Martin may appear as if I don't appreciate his observations about faith. He presents useful arguments about people seeking God in their lives. But I still think he tends to be a bit too simplistic in his approach.

The Path of Disbelief is one that many intellectuals embark upon. They want absolute intellectual proof that there is a God. According to Martin, the intellect can often be an obstacle to faith because it closes a person's heart to God's presence. I can sympathize with intellectuals. They don't trust their feelings. Feeling that God is present at a certain moment in your life doesn't necessarily mean he is present. We may simply be imagining it. There are many people who need more than a "feeling" about God: they need to be convinced *intellectually*.

Martin's hero, Thomas Merton, came to God through the intellect when he read Etienne Gilson's book *The Spirit of Medieval Philosophy*. Within its pages, Merton finally discovered a definition of God that appealed to his intellect. Prior to reading it, Merton was essentially an agnostic if not atheistic. If Merton had not come across Gilson, I wonder if he would have ever become a Christian.

The Path of Return addresses people who once believed in God and were members of a church, but left because they experienced something that seemed to deny the existence of God. In Martin's case, it was the tragic death of a friend in a car accident. He could not reconcile such a meaningless tragedy with a benign, loving God, and for a time left behind his church and faith. An off-the-cuff remark by a friend about his friend's death, one concerning the mystery of suffering, helped him return to the path of belief.

The Path of Exploration concerns people who explore all of the world's religions. No religion is excluded: one can study everything from Buddhism to Quakerism. The problem, Martin argues, with this path is that it can reduce a person to becoming an explorer for the rest of his/her life: "your entire life may become one of exploration—

constant sampling, spiritual grazing." Again, I must differ with Martin. Some of the holiest people I've ever met have been such explorers. I have found them to be far more kind, tolerant, and wise than many of my Catholic friends, including the many Religious I know, among them monks who have lived in monasteries most of their adult lives. Explorers often do find wisdom, but it's the wisdom of the ages, from all cultures: rather than rendering them narrow-minded and pompous as if they have all the answers to life's problems, they realize that there are as many ways to God as there are people.

The Path of Confusion is the path Martin knows very well. He admits to being a very confused young man. Although he was raised as a Catholic, he describes his family's Catholicism as "lukewarm." I like his honesty here. I too grew up in such a family. He was knocked off this path rather dramatically when he just happened to turn on the TV while a documentary about Thomas Merton was being aired. Merton's face radiated a peace that totally captivated Martin. He then went out to purchase Merton's autobiography. I fully understand the impact a book can have on one's life: It can transform a life, and Merton's book seemingly did so for Martin.

So we now return to Martin's original comment: faith is a gift from God. Okay, maybe he's right. It's rather mysterious that Martin at that very moment in his life would speak to his friend about the death of his college friend, and she'd say just the right remark to put him back on the path of belief. It's rather mysterious that Martin would just at that moment turn on TV when a program about Merton was airing, and this program would lead him to becoming a Jesuit priest. Coincidences? I always remember Jung's comment, "There are no coincidences." If it's true, then my writing this book must have a purpose I know nothing about because the idea of this book didn't come from me. And here I am writing it—about a man I barely know! Well, I'm getting to know him....

Martin believes that we all have an innate desire for God, a risky pronouncement for there are many people who would demand that he prove this idea, but in fact, one can't prove it. Either one believes it, or one doesn't. He argues his point rather convincingly, employing seven common ways by which a desire for God reveals itself:

Incompletion
Common Longings and Connections
Uncommon Longings
Exaltation
Clarity
Desire to Follow
Desire for Holiness
Vulnerability

Before I comment on these intriguing categories, it has just occurred to me what a fine Catholic apologist Martin is. No doubt about it: Martin is out to win over his readers not only to Ignatian spirituality but also to God and Catholicism. And to be quite blunt about it, he's not very subtle about his intentions. Thomas Merton and Henri Nouwen were also Catholic apologists, but they were subtle about it. In fact, their very subtlety attracted many non-Catholics to their writing. I'm wondering if Martin's following is primarily Catholic because one can't help being reminded on each page of his book that he is a Catholic priest, and a Jesuit one at that! Let's not forget that many people have over the ages been suspicious of what has often been described as Jesuitical tactics; in fact, in our English language the very word

Jesuitical has attained a pejorative connotation. To prove my point, I looked up the word *Jesuit* on the Internet:

> 1. a member of the Society of Jesus, a Roman Catholic religious order for men, founded by Ignatius Loyola in 1534. 2. a crafty schemer; cunning dissembler; casuist: a hostile and offensive term.

Should Martin be more subtle? I don't think it would make any difference because his books sell, and in the publishing business selling and profit are the bottom line. I'm not quite sure who his following actually is. He may indeed have many non-Catholic admirers.

While I'm on the subject of Catholic apologetics, I must praise Martin for his orderly presentation of ideas. Although he's not as subtle as I would wish him to be, he is far from slipshod: he is meticulous in presenting his ideas, and he backs them up with allusions to other famous writers on spirituality. In this chapter alone, he refers to both spiritual and secular writers: Ruth Burrows, Henri Nouwen, Gerard Manley Hopkins, Karl Rahner, Julian Barnes, Abraham Joshua Heschel, and Evelyn Waugh. He is a man/priest who is well versed and well read. You have to be if you want to win people to your way of thinking and living.

I also admire his convictions. If you have come across a "treasure," and if you are altruistic, you want to share your treasure with others. Martin believes he has achieved worthy, wise insights into life, and being altruistic, he wants to share them with others. And let's face it, all he can do is present his treasures, no one has to accept them. You either embrace them or ignore them. On second thought, you can *question* them until you finally decide whether you will embrace or ignore them.

Incompletion. This is the classic feeling of a man or woman living without God. It's also an assumption. Does a Christian have the right to presume that if one isn't a member of a church or if one doesn't believe in God, one feels incomplete? Many a famous person has argued incompletion, including St. Augustine, who famously said, "Our hearts are restless until they rest in Thee." I happen to know, however, many people who espouse no God or church, and they appear as happy as the next fellow, often possessing a greater life force than many a Catholic I know, including myself.

As Christians, I think we can become a bit smug, concluding that only people who follow our way of life can be happy. Well, it's not the case. Many people find completion in their families, in their work, in their social lives, in their pursuits of hobbies and cultural affairs. They are also involved in philanthropic activities, all done without stimulus from the Bible or their minister or priest: they believe that they're doing the right thing.

But Martin is correct to argue that many people indeed turn to God because of feelings of incompletion. It's a pervasive feeling in our secular society, especially in America, which started out as a theocracy under Puritan law in New England. To underscore his argument, he mentions the singer Peggy Lee's famous existential song, "Is That All There Is?" I remember when I first heard her sing it. I enjoyed her singing style but hated the message of the song because all it offered as an answer to the question "Is that all there is?" is to party, and "have a ball," or as we colloquially say, "eat, drink, and be merry." Such a philosophy was prevalent during the 1960s and 1970s, but I don't think it satisfied too many people, and the so-called cultural revolution of the 1960s quickly dissolved. To be fair, some good changes in our way of life came of it. Americans aren't such prudes sexually; they also more quickly and rightfully question political and religious authority, and they have learned that they are truly free to choose the life they want to live; no one can force them to live in a certain way. All that's good. Even Catholics mustered the courage to question the church, which they had rarely done before Vatican II. Today because of the sexual scandals, the laity is questioning boldly and more often. The groundwork for such was established during the 1960s.

Common Longings and Connections. Again this title is another assumption in order to make a point: Martin believes all people have a common longing for God, one with which we are born. It's a sweeping general statement that can't be proved. But it's a common feeling to have for the kind of a person Martin is. Let's face it, he lived his life within a family of faith (although "lukewarm" faith), and most of the people in his life were believers, and if they aren't, we Catholics usually categorize them as people who really long to believe but can't.

To support his argument, Martin quotes the famous novelist Julian Barnes in his recent memoir, *Nothing to Be Afraid Of*: "I miss the God who inspired Italian painting and French stained glass, German music and English chapter houses, and those tumbledown heaps of stone on Celtic headlands which were once symbolic beacons in the darkness and storm."

Missing something is not necessarily a longing for something. Barnes no longer believes in God. He still lives a useful, creative, fascinating life as a man, husband and novelist. He has looked at life without a belief in God, and what has he found? He still finds life to be beautiful and worth living. As for beauty, in the past, the church was a patron of the arts. Today it no longer is, but art is still being created. Yes, the art may be different because today most people can read and write whereas before the church created art for a mostly uneducated laity. What better way to tell the story of Christ than through the beauty of stained-glass windows at which the peasants could with wonder gaze?

Is there, then, within men and women a universal longing to believe in God? I can't answer that question, actually no one can. An affirmative answer, however, could easily be argued because every great culture that has ever blossomed on earth has had at its center religion with a god or gods at its head.

Uncommon Longings. Another way our longing for God is revealed is through mystical feelings. There are times, Martin argues, when we have intense feelings that God is present; such feelings fall under the aegis of what Jesuit theology calls "everyday mysticism." This feeling of God's presence is, Martin says, "unmistakable." On such occasions, we are lifted up from our usual way of perceiving the world. His description reminds me of William Wordsworth's ode, "Intimations of Immortality." Again, we are discussing feelings or intimations. The latter are not scientific; thus, there is no way to prove what they intimate. Yet literature is filled with such descriptions of men and women who momentarily feel God's presence, usually through the beauty of nature or art. I'm reminded of the French mystic Simone Weil, who felt God's presence through the beauty of Gregorian chant. Henri Nouwen felt it through the beauty of Rembrandt's painting. The poet Mary Oliver felt it through the beauty of Cape Cod's flora and fauna. Martin himself felt it as a boy when he was stopped in his tracks by the beauty of a meadowland, one filled with so much life and beauty that he felt that God was calling to him.

Simone Weil's theory, as mentioned, is that God uses beauty to lure people to him. I find her theory a rather intriguing one. Dostoevsky believed that "beauty would save the world." Martin argues that we shouldn't dismiss such feelings, such longings. So even though they can't be put under a microscope or analyzed scientifically, we should take them seriously. They fall under what the church often describes as "mystery," those inexplicable feelings. Let's face it, there are so many things in life that fall beneath the penumbra of the mystery, and although I'm uneasy in employing this explanation too often, I am humble enough to accept it. I would be a fool to do otherwise, and I'm sure there are still plenty of my former teachers out there who wouldn't be loath to say so!

Exaltation. Sometimes in life, we not only experience beauty that moves or lifts us to another degree of consciousness, but we actually feel invaded by a Power that surges through us. It can be frightening and/or uplifting. He gives us an example of W. H. Auden, who was sitting with friends when he was overcome by a tremendous love for his friends: "I felt their existence as themselves to be of infinite value and rejoiced in it."

What is interesting about this experience of Exaltation is that it is not only reserved for saints and mystics. It can happen to anyone. I myself once experienced it while I was conducting an examination of one of my classes. As I walked up and down the aisles watching my students quickly scribble their answers to the exam questions, I was overwhelmed with love for all of them. I saw them spiritually in their innocent beauty; their attention studiously fixed upon the test rendered each unconsciously egoless. I found myself bemused by my feelings for them, for this class was not easy to control, among whom were students who were a handful to control on a daily basis. But for one shining moment, I felt love for each one of them, as if I were seeing them in a different light, dare I say "divine" light? Or as a Platonist like novelist Iris Murdoch, I was seeing them Platonically. Either way it was an extraordinary experience, one I still vividly recall.

Clarity. This feeling many people can identify with. It's not complicated. It's the feeling that the English poet Alexander Pope caught so well in his maxim, "God's in his heaven and all's right with the world." It's a moment of clearness, when one believes that all is as it should be. It's also similar to William Blake's verse, one Thomas Merton fell in love with and reworded: "Everything that is/Is holy." I can't argue with this insight.

Desire to Follow. Some people are overcome by a desire to follow Christ. By *follow*, Martin means action that demands sacrifice; he is referring to those people who are called to follow Christ in religious life, a distinct minority if one considers the number of people who populate the world. But this feeling to follow Christ also applies to laypeople, for there are many laypeople who have offered their lives to Christ.

I begin my morning by having coffee in my study, which overlooks Church Street, called such because at the end of the street is Holy Name Catholic Church, my parish church. Without fail, I observe daily a gray-haired woman in her sixties pass my house at 7:45 a.m. on the dot. I know she must attend the 8:00 a.m. Mass at my church because at about 8:30 a.m., she again passes my house on her return to her own home. One can time one's watch by her coming and going. She is a follower of Christ, and it's likely she's what we call a daily communicant. I myself sometimes feel guilty that I'm not walking down the street with her to Mass, but I write best in the morning and don't want to impede my quotidian Muse.

As to following: I can remember my mother's warning me to be my own person and not to follow the crowd. Yes, it's good advice. But sometimes it can be a fine way of action, that is, to be a follower. To be a follower of Christ: well, I can't think of anything finer.

Desire for Holiness. Martin believes that holiness is good for it attracts us to God. Holy people have indeed inspired me. How do I know they're holy? Well, holiness has its own aura; one just "feels" when someone is holy (and again, it's a feeling that can't be proved). In my own life, I've met several people who, I believe, were saints. One is my paternal grandmother, a daily communicant. I vividly recall visiting her. She would want me all to herself, so she'd invite me into her bedroom where I would sit in a chair, and she'd tell me stories of her life in Ireland when she was a young girl. Her room was like a chapel, with statues of the saints, the Blessed Mother, and of course, Jesus. In front of many of them, she had vigil lights, their small candles aflame. So many flames in one small room scared me! I'll never forget the ambience of her room; it *felt* holy and my grandmother emanated holiness. I never met anyone so kind, so accepting, so tolerant, so people loving. She was totally non-judgmental. I didn't know the word at the time, but Grandmother exhibited what I now know is Agapetic Love: Unconditional Love.

Another instance of meeting holiness in a person was a monk I'd met at the Trappist abbey here in Massachusetts. I was in the habit of retreating once a year at St. Joseph's Abbey in Spencer. I don't remember the particulars of how I became engaged in a conversation with this particular monk, but we sat in the retreat office talking one day. As we were conversing, I was overwhelmed with a feeling that I was in the presence of a saint. He was a short, unassuming man in his eighties. He talked about his life growing up in Brooklyn, and I was simply fascinated. Then he suddenly asked me if I had any questions to ask him, and after a brief reflection, I dared to ask him if he had ever regretted becoming a monk. He beamed a smile, "Never a regret." And I knew in my bones he meant it. His brief answer was so certain, so profound. I'll never forget that short exchange between a young man in his twenties and a monk in his eighties.

Holiness is not always overt. Often it's hidden. I believe we likely come into contact with many holy people, but because we don't possess any kind of radar system to alert us, we meet them unaware of their proximity to God. On the other hand, haven't we all met a few "holier-than-thou" types? How insufferable they are, but compassion must come into play on such occasions, although I must admit I sometimes haven't been so kind. Alas, my own lack of holiness!

Vulnerability. Martin's final way: God can lure us to him when we are vulnerable—through illness, through the death of a loved one, though a great disappointment. Martin believes that when our defenses are down, God has a better "opening" to communicate with us. It's what happened to Ignatius of Loyola: when he was recuperating from war wounds, he listened to the "still, small voice" of God.

I recall the maxim about there being no atheists in foxholes. I personally don't like Martin's argument because to turn to God because one is under duress seems to me, at least, too self-serving, too ego-driven. It's why I loathe the Pascalian Wager idea: There's a fifty-fifty chance that there is indeed a God, and if at death, there is no God and no afterlife, then you won't know it and won't lose anything. But if there is and you've lived a good life according to the laws of God and the church, you'll be the beneficiary of salvation and the Beatific Vision. You've won the lottery!

I respect belief in God far more than that. Belief must arise from the depths of our minds and souls. It's the only kind of faith I trust. Belief based on our being vulnerable is one I'll take a pass on. But to be fair to Martin's argument, suffering does indeed cause many people to take stock of their lives, and it may lead to conversion. And if it works for that person, who am I to dismiss it? As the maxim says: God works in *mysterious* ways.

There you have it: but it all really comes down to Mystery, does it not? Who knows truly why one person believes in God and another doesn't? It can't be explained but, of course, as human beings we have intellects; thus, we try to nail down such beliefs with/by thought. But in my gut, I believe that faith transcends thought as well as feelings. It is indeed one of the great Mysteries of life.

Martin offers excellent advice in his chapter "Friendship with God." He lists the ways we can develop our divine friendship:

Spending Time
Learning
Being Honest
Listening
Listening Carefully
Changing
Being Silent

Spending time. As with human friendship, we must invest time, our most valued commodity. We have to *be* there for our friends, which means we must take time out of our busy days to keep in touch with friends—by phone, by e-mail, by getting together socially, by being available to friends who are going through difficult times. Perhaps we may have to offer help either financially or psychologically. Friendship means giving, not taking.

Martin argues that the same philosophy applies to God: we need to set time aside in our often overcrowded lives for God, which can be done in many ways: morning prayer, attending Mass, short prayers during the day, evening prayer, reading books that address the spiritual life, reading the Bible. But again, these acts require that we *invest our time* in them. Martin says, "Prayer is being attentive to God." Yes, I agree. It always comes down to attention. In my definition of prayer, I am more in sync with Simone Weil than Ignatius: When you pay attention, fixing your unmixed, undivided attention on something Other, the ego temporarily disappears. When this happens, it is called prayer.

Learning. How do we *learn* about God? Martin suggests the best way is to read the scriptures, something for which Catholics are not well known. Non-Catholics know the Bible better than Catholics, no doubt about it. My Protestant friends can quote chapter and verse of the Bible. I can't. There are some parts of the Bible I know well, but I never really had much Bible education, and I went to Catholic schools for thirteen years!

Why so little emphasis on the Bible? The great taboo is individual interpretation, about which the church is emphatic, for only she has the right to interpret the Bible, no individual does. Well, it's what I was taught, and it's still the position of the Church. For example, I remember interpreting a parable to my religion teacher in high school, an interpretation rejected by my instructor. When I asked why, I'll never forget her response, "Robert, can you quote authority to support your interpretation?" I intuitively knew she meant the church, and I humbly replied, "No"—end of discussion.

Being honest. As in our human friendships, we must be honest with friends, not afraid to speak our minds, to express our true feelings. Martin encourages us to be honest with God: even if it means telling him off if we become angry. To support such unusual counsel, he quotes Jesuit Gerard Manley Hopkins's sonnet, "Thou Art Indeed Just, Lord." In this poem, Hopkins lets God know how disappointed he is in God. Hopkins has done everything according to the book, obeyed God's laws and the church's laws, practiced penance, prayed, and yet everything he does ends in "disappointment" while at the same time he observes others, who are far from holy, prosper. And he's damn mad about it! Hopkins is trapped in what is often called a spiritually arid period, and he poignantly calls out to God, "Mine, O thou Lord of life, send my roots rain." This verse I fell in love with many years ago, for it is the lament of so many of us Catholics who

85

yearn for some consolation in our spiritual lives, but often have to be satisfied with very little—or nothing at all.

I remember when I shared my own aridity with a Trappist monk, begging him to help me get through a rough time. He couldn't help me much so I asked him what did he do when he experienced aridity. I'll never forget his response, "Nothing, I just wait it out." I was surprised because I thought he'd say pray more. But after later reflection, I realized that waiting is a kind of prayer. In the end, it's really all we can do. It's all Hopkins could do. This poem, by the way, is often referred to as one of Hopkins's Terrible Sonnets, poems about an agonizing time he spent while teaching in Dublin, Ireland.

Listening. Martin believes that listening is an important part of creating a friendship with God. In fact, he says friendship "requires" listening. If one person does all the talking, then there is no true communication. In our modern culture, to find a good listener is like finding a needle in a haystack. Let's be candid, most people want to hog the conversation by talking about *themselves*! To truly listen to another person demands that you forget yourself: the Other must become the object of your complete, unmixed attention. How many people in our ego-driven culture are willing to give themselves over completely to another person by keeping their mouths shut and listening?

With God it's hard because his voice is low: "The still, small voice of God." To hear God you need to listen ever so carefully. You need to include silence in your life. You need also to include solitude, not to say that God won't speak to you unless you are silent and alone, but it's more likely that you will *hear* God more clearly (and more often) if you include silence and solitude in your life, with which all mystics agree.

Martin also encourages people to imagine having a conversation with God. Here, again, I balk. To imagine what God would say to you is really to imagine what *you* would say. It's not the kind of counsel I'd pass on to anyone if I were a spiritual advisor.

Listening Carefully. By listening carefully, Martin again means a kind of exquisite attention. This kind of listening can be very rewarding because it can result in the attainment of *insights* that can help us live our lives, achieve self-knowledge and intimacy with God.

How is it that out of the blue, it seems, we have insights that allow us to solve problems in our familial, social, spiritual, and psychological lives? Well, often such insights are the result of a goodly amount of time that we have spent in silence and solitude with God. They are God's answers to our prayers. And often, when these life-changing insights arrive, we find ourselves saying, "Why didn't I realize this before? It's so obvious." It's evident because one's "doors of perception" have been cleansed by careful listening. Rather ironic in a way: that careful *listening* can help us with *seeing* better.

Changing. Our relationship with God, if it's a real one, will change: the God of our youth will not be the God of our adulthood. The God of our thirties will not be the God of our sixties. Our human friendships endure all kinds of shifts and changes, ones that sometimes shake the very foundations of our friendships, but rather than destroy friendship they strengthen it. Same with God.

For example, in my young life God was a patriarchal figure, a God of law and order, and watch out if you break any of his rules! As I grew older and read more and reflected more, I realized that God is not so much a God of Law and Order but one of Love. For me the most revealing book on this subject was *The Revelations of Divine Love* by Lady Julian of Norwich. She opened my eyes to God's Agapetic Love: God's Unconditional Love for each of us. I wish I had known about agapetic love when I was a teenager because then I was so terrified of God. To be afraid of God, in my opinion, is not to know God.

If you are afraid of God, you cannot have a true friendship with him. You may have a relationship with him but not friendship.

Being Silent. Martin believes it's one of the best ways toward friendship and intimacy with God. For the first time he admits that listening is far more important than talking, so his advice on having conversations with God is somewhat nullified. And I agree with his advice.

I like Martin's succinct advice: to connect with God, one must sometimes disconnect with the world. Shut off the phone, TV, computer, cell phone, BlackBerry, and iPod. I just read in the newspaper of a summer camp that forbids kids from bringing along with them their toys: by which they mean all the just mentioned items. The attendance list fell dramatically. Seems that kids today aren't so much interested in swimming, hiking, boating, canoeing, archery, and all the other camplike activities I remember doing as a kid. My goodness, even our kids can't slow down and smell the roses.

As for being close to nature: when a child would rather sit in front of a computer than swim in a beautiful lake rimmed by a forest or climb a magnificent mountain, I am dumbfounded. But to be candid, I'm out of touch with today's youth. Their values are radically different from mine—a narrative for another book.

Martin himself is a talker. He's a guest on many talk shows, he writes for *America*, and he's pursued by many for his opinions on controversial subjects like celibacy, pedophilia, and modern spirituality. His answers to so many questions have come, I believe, from the many hours he has spent in prayer and reflection as a Religious. There is a time for everything under the sun: a time for silence, and a time for speaking. Martin is speaking, for his order and for his church as he should be.

Another large, eye-catching ad of Martin's book in *America* with a complimentary blurb from *Commonweal*. I'm glad he's getting such good reviews. As I know all too well, a good review can enormously help to sell a book, a bad one able to destroy it. It's the reason why I am always amazed that some reviewers can be so cavalierly cruel in their opinions, not taking into consideration that behind every book there is a human being with feelings, a person who may have spent a great portion of his/her life on a book. And the ad again renders me very envious. To have had an ad like that for one of my books! Alas, it's something I'll likely never experience.

There are people who write quickly and can put a book out yearly. Martin seems to be a writer of this sort. There are writers who painstakingly compose their work, perfectionists who agonize over a word, even a comma. For that person then to receive a savage review, well, I know writers who've been made physically and psychologically ill from negative reviews. I think of novelists May Sarton and Doris Grumbach, both of whom were the recipients of unfair, hostile reviews in important newspapers, and therefore their novels were doomed and made no money. Such is life, I guess. But Martin is fortunate, for at this moment in time, he's the Golden Boy of American Catholicism. A great burden for him to carry, for his every word and action will be scrutinized. It happened to Merton and to Fulton Sheen, and both paid dearly, being resoundingly knocked off their pedestal by their own: by other Catholics who didn't share their opinions and who possessed the power to harm them, and they did.

I've just finished Martin's chapter, "God Meets You Where You Are." It's primarily a chapter explaining Ignatian spirituality. In this kind of spirituality, you "compose the place" of your meditation on the Bible by using your imagination: you imagine yourself in a biblical scene or in God's presence and take a part in it. You are like an actor in a play. Martin insists that God can indeed speak to you through your imagination, or rather Ignatius insists on this methodology and Martin repeats it.

Martin stresses the point that in Ignatius's life the imagination had a greater impact on the saint's life than analytical thinking: his imagination was the power that drove his spiritual life, fine for Ignatius, and for people who follow the Ignatian way. I'm not attracted to Ignatius's method because there is too much ego involved. In our deepest prayer, the self (ego) should disappear; thus, any kind of methodology that places too much emphasis on the "I" being present in an imagined scene is suspect to me.

Merton dropped the Ignatian method rather early in his conversion. He too saw its flaw. But, again, it's a matter of opinion, for there are many Catholics who attend Ignatian retreats. But these retreats are usually one-on-one retreats with the retreatant reporting daily to a priest (often a Jesuit or someone trained in the Ignatian method). Professor Paul Mariani has written a rather interesting book on his Ignatian retreat, *Thirty Days: On Retreat with the Exercises of St. Ignatius*, but I remember while reading it that it's the kind of retreat I'd never choose to engage in myself. There's far too much self-scrutiny. I prefer a group retreat with its communal atmosphere and opportunity to connect with our brothers and sisters in Christ.

As I see it, here is the Ignatian flaw: in imagining a biblical scene, YOU are in charge as producer, director, and actor. Yet I cannot rule out that behind all three is the inspiration of the Holy Spirit, leading you beyond the limits of your imagination and ego.

I checked Merton's autobiography about his flirtation with Ignatius's *Spiritual Exercises*, which he read in his New York City apartment. He scrupulously followed Ignatius's directions even to darkening his room by pulling down the blinds so that there was just enough light for him to see the pages and to gaze upon the crucifix on the wall over his bed.

He thought, however, that Jesuits would suffer a shock if they had seen him sitting cross-legged on the floor like Mahatma Gandhi. He admits that, without the direction of a Jesuit, he likely missed out on the big, simple, and radical truths of the *Spiritual Exercises*. But he docilely followed all of St. Ignatius's rules about "composition of place" and confessed that he had indeed gotten closer to the Holy Family through its practice—yet I wonder, for Merton wrote his autobiography during the first fervor of his conversion: he wasn't about to criticize any Catholic saint!

There was also a theological point that made a deep impression on him. He already possessed a horror of mortal sin, but through the *Exercises* he also clearly saw the malice of venial sin and decided that sin of any sort was to follow one's will rather than God's will, for whom we were created.

It should be noted that, except for his autobiography, Merton rarely again refers to Ignatius or his *Spiritual Exercises*. As to religious orders, during his time of choice, he, at first, preferred the Franciscan order, but they rescinded his admittance when he admitted to fathering a child in England. It was then, because of a recommendation of a friend, Merton turned his attention to the Trappists, who quickly accepted him as a postulant. I doubt that any seminary today would accept him after his admitting fathering a child. We like to think we are more accepting, tolerant, and modern today than in the past, but in this regard I don't believe we've made much progress—few religious orders or seminaries today would allow him admission, particularly now because of the church's sex scandal, a grievously unhappy chapter in the history of the church.

Martin's chapter "Surrendering to the Future" is about Obedience, Acceptance, and Suffering. Here we see Martin the Catholic apologist at his best. Who could render blind obedience better than a Jesuit?

He flat-out admits that Ignatius is "crystal clear" about obedience: "All should strongly dispose themselves to observe obedience and to distinguish themselves in it, not only in the matters of obligation but also in the others, even though nothing else be perceived except an indication of the superior's will without an expressed command." In other words, a Jesuit just knowing his superior's intention is sufficient reason to demand obedience.

Martin reveals that the word *obedience* derives from the Latin, *oboedire*, which includes the root for "to hear." Thus, obedience is a matter of hearing; therefore, this virtue should help us spiritually to follow Jesus' example: he who *listened* to and was *obedient* to God the Father.

I could argue forever that I don't agree with blind obedience. For instance, if you are a Jesuit, you do *exactly* as you are told; you *never* question your superiors, you *always* obey. The argument in favor of such blind obedience is that the Holy Spirit *inspires* religious superiors, that they, indeed, know what's best for you and for your spiritual life. But who is to say all superiors listen to the Holy Spirit?

For instance, I believe the church's sex scandal today is the result of such blind obedience. But it is still such a sensitive issue, and I'll not belabor it because the church is still reeling from it. I believe everyone, however, has the right to question authority, and everyone has the right to follow his own conscience.

Martin offers two Jesuit examples of men who practiced "holy" obedience. The first is Father John Drinan, SJ, who for many years represented my state of Massachusetts in the U.S. House of Representatives. When Pope John Paul ordered Drinan not to run again for Congress, Drinan quickly obeyed. I remember the outrage there was in Massachusetts, for Drinan had represented our state with honor, always on the side of the disenfranchised. We lost much when he left politics. (How ironic because John Paul II was, behind the scenes, very involved in Polish politics and secretly involved with President Reagan, causing the fall of the Communist regime and literally of the Berlin Wall).

But Father Drinan had no choice. If he disobeyed, he could have been ousted from the Jesuits or suffered excommunication. When one has no choice, is that also obedience? Martin's view of Drinan's actions is that he is admirable, but as I see it, he was *forced* to "obey": it was not a matter of *free will*, an intrinsic quality that the church has always insisted that we possess in addition to the intrinsic right every Catholic possesses to follow his own conscience.

Another example of "admirable" obedience is theologian John Courtney Murray, who was silenced by the church because he believed that people had the right to worship God as they pleased, not congruent with Catholic teaching, and consequently suspended as an official Catholic theologian. Murray didn't protest, and as Martin writes, he returned all the books on the subject to the library of Woodstock College.

However, having a friend in Cardinal Spellman (it's not what you know but who you know!), Murray was appointed to the Second Vatican Council as an official *peritus* or expert and later celebrated Mass with Pope Paul VI, a public sign of Murray's official "rehabilitation." But was he really rehabilitated? Had he really changed his opinion? Or had he just learned to keep his mouth shut? The point

Martin is cleverly highlighting is that if you obey, down the line you may indeed be rewarded. A specious argument to say the least, but I do understand the exigencies of religious life: life in the church is as political as life in the world.

So what really is good about obedience? I think Martin gets it right when he writes about Walter Ciszek, an American-born Jesuit priest who volunteered to go to Poland in 1939. To make a long story short, Ciszek ended up being arrested by the Russians and sent to fifteen years of hard labor in Siberia. Many believed that Ciszek had died, but with the help of President Kennedy, he was released from prison, and he arrived at the Jesuit *America* office in 1963. When he was asked how he survived such a tortured life, his short answer was "Divine Providence." His longer answer is found in his two books about living in a Soviet labor camp; it can be reduced to one word: Obedience. Ciszek believed that the life that he was offered was the will of God. Thus, he embraced it. He explains that figuring out God's will isn't difficult: it's presented to us every day when we wake up. The life we have to live that day is God's will for us. Simple as that. Thus, obedience means accepting the reality of our lives, but we still have the free will to choose our life's reality; no one has the right to tell us otherwise.

Martin takes on the troubling subject of suffering. He's not foolish enough to try to explain why people suffer. The only solace he can offer the suffering is to remind them that in suffering God is with them. The why of suffering, the degree of it, and to whom it happens falls under the umbrella of Mystery. Martin makes it clear that each person can have his or her own perspective on suffering, but the best way to face and endure suffering is to accept it as God's will. Why, every sufferer asks, does God ask us to suffer? Again, the only safe answer to offer anyone is "Mystery."

Ignatius's answer to suffering is a bit different. He teaches that the best way to face suffering is to emulate Christ: Jesus *accepts* the suffering that he was given, saying, "Not My will but Thine be done."

There is always that haunting cry that Christendom can never adequately fathom, "My God, My God, why hast thou forsaken me?" And there are so many attempts at explaining his cry that for me it definitely falls under the umbrella of Mystery. And yet I must be frank: I still find this answer not to be satisfactory.

I enjoyed Martin's insights about the theme of vocation in his chapter "Be Who You Is!" Two of the very important questions we all have, at some point in our lives, to answer are "What should I do?" and "Who should I be?"

He makes the point that the word *vocation* derives from the Latin *vocare*, meaning to call. For a long time, the word *vocation* was only considered to refer to religious calling, for example, to be a nun or a priest. But ever since the Second Vatican Council, the church has emphasized that everyone has a vocation, whether it be religious or secular. I myself considered becoming a teacher because I believed I was *called* to be a teacher. I never really viewed it as a job. In fact, I always considered teaching not as an occupation but as a spiritual call to action. I still do. But more and more our society has truly reduced teaching to a job, similar to an assembly-line job. Instead of cars coming down the line, it's just another group of kids, and teachers are required to stuff them with enough information to pass tests, and voilà! they are educated!

Martin emphasizes that vocation is linked to desire, but he also believes that one's particular vocation isn't so much about finding it as its being revealed to you.

Martin chronicles his own search for vocation. He had a number of jobs before becoming a Jesuit, but he insists that all jobs can serve as a way of finding God. In fact, he believes God must be found in *everything*. Jobs, for instance, can be a means toward a higher goal. For example, people who work in the caring of children or the elderly are in a position to do much good. Yes, they get paid to do what they do, but what is more important is *how* you take care of them.

Which reminds me of the nursing home where my mother lived in her last year. I was amazed at the difference among nurses. Some were so kind, gentle, and caring with their patients. Others weren't. In fact, some were unkind, harsh, and uncaring. Same with the nursing aides; some were exemplary in the way they handled the sick elderly, others were sometimes rough, impatient, and in one case I observed, harshly insensitive.

No matter what vocation or job we choose, Martin says, we have to bring our best self to it— meaning our ethical values and our spiritual beliefs. Our inner self cannot be separated from our outer self, which also means that we must bring our conscience to our jobs.

He also emphasizes the *dignity* of work. It is intrinsically dignified, but it becomes more dignified by the attitude we bring to it. I remember my own mother saying (she must have said it thousands of times, or so it seems to me now) that if you do anything, do it well, and that meant the small and the big actions. On a small scale, it may mean washing a window until it sparkles. I remember my washing windows. We had an apartment so it meant my sitting on the ledge outside and being very careful not to fall. I was quite proud finishing a rather dirty window when mother arrived to inspect my work. She shook her head. "You missed a spot," she said, pointing to a corner of the window. I looked, and she was right, but I was furious that she didn't applaud my work on the rest of the window. Later, when she returned for further inspection, I received a smile. It dissipated my anger, but her reaction underscored what she always repeated, if you do something, do it well. Don't skim, don't shortchange. Give it your all—even if it's only a window!

Sometimes we perform our best, and it doesn't seem to matter to anyone, seemingly even God. Martin offers Gerard Manley Hopkins as an example. Hopkins tried his best to be a good teacher at University College, Dublin. But no matter how hard he tried, he was in the end a failure, a fact that took its toll on him by causing him to descend into a terrible depression which nearly destroyed him.

Martin's solution to such a dilemma is for people to simply hand over to God the fruits of their labor and let God do with it what he will. Well, of course, it's easy to say, but it's difficult to practice.

Vocation involves, however, more than just *doing*; it also refers to *being*. We shouldn't allow a vocation to change who we truly are. Martin refers to the vocational mask: don't fall into the trap of believing the mask is the real you. Learn to drop the mask at the end of the day and certainly don't bring it home with you.

He reminds us that God loves us as we are, which is vital to remember. We may have to prove certain actions to our superiors and bosses, but when it comes to God, we don't have to prove anything. We need only *be* ourselves. At the same time, we must try to understand that God indeed wants us to become a certain kind of person. Martin's spiritual director once counseled him not to let anyone take from him the freedom to become who God wants him to be.

After much writing about what vocation is, what it means in our lives, how can it affect the way we live? Martin's final advice is astoundingly brief but profound. He says, "First, remember that God

97

loves you. Second, realize that God loves you as an individual, not simply in the abstract. Third, accept your desires, skills, and talents as things *given to you by God* for your happiness and for others. These are gifts from the Creator. Fourth, avoid the temptation to compare yourself to others and denigrate or undervalue yourself. Fifth, *move away* from actions that are sinful or that keep you from being compassionate, loving, and free. Sixth, trust that *God will help you* because God desires for you to become who you are meant to be. Seventh, recognize that the process of becoming the person you are meant to be is a *long process* and can take time."

Excellent advice!

I've now completed reading Martin's *The Jesuit Guide to (Almost) Everything.* I enjoyed the book, but what I will remember most about the book has little to do with Jesuits, Ignatius of Loyola, or Ignatian spirituality. What I will remember is a vignette about Martin when he was a boy, so beautifully and simply narrated that he renders it unforgettable in lyrical prose, an experience he had written about before.

When James was a boy, he used to ride his bike to school in the morning and back home in the afternoon. Usually he would ride with friends, but he sometimes rode alone. There was something exhilarating about sailing down leaf-arched streets, down the clean sidewalks and under the orange morning sun with the wind blowing through his hair and whistling past his ears.

One morning, he stopped, got off his big blue Schwinn to walk down a path that led to a set of six steps. At the top of the stairs lay one of his favorite places in his world: from this place he could see "a broad meadow, bordered on the left by tall oak trees and on the right by baseball fields. And in each season of the year it was beautiful."

One spring morning when he was ten or eleven, he stopped to catch his breath while walking through the meadow before his school. Let's now let him narrate:

> The bike's metal basket, packed with my schoolbooks, swung violently to one side, and I almost lost my homework to the grasshoppers. Standing astride my bike, I could see so much going on around me—so much color, so much activity, so much *life*.
>
> Looking toward the school on the brow of the hill, I felt an overwhelming happiness. I felt so happy to be alive. And I felt a fantastic longing: to both possess and be a part of what was around me. I can still see myself standing in this meadow, surrounded by creation, more clearly than almost any other memory from childhood.

I would categorize his experience as a mystical one. Some would say that his experience more accurately falls under a Wordsworthian moment of being. They may be correct. There is a loss of the self in the beauty of what is before him. Thus, one could describe his experience as an aesthetic one. But the longing to be a part of what is before him illustrates a desire (or to use his word "longing") for the mystical unitive experience, to chance the loss of the ego. He doesn't use the word *God* in any of his descriptions, but he does use the word *creation*, which is a loaded word implying a Creator (God).

Strict interpreters of what a mystical experience is would argue with me, saying that I am being too free with the word *mystical*. I beg to differ, but to diffuse debate I will concede that James stood at the edge of the *transcendental* life. As the mystic Richard Rolle would say, the "heavenly door" was definitely ajar for James, and the young boy was permitted a glimpse of the Eternal, but because he was still very much *James*, and there was not a complete loss of selfhood, Martin could not claim (and he doesn't) a mystical experience. But to come to the very edge, well, it's quite extraordinary for a young boy.

You may ask why I'm emphasizing his experience, one many of us have had at least once in our lifetime (I'm sad for those who've never experienced it). The reason is that his experience reminds me of another one that is recorded in Father Bede Griffiths's beautiful autobiography, *The Golden String*. Let me share it with you so that you can compare the two. Griffiths was walking with *his* bike through his school playing fields. He writes:

> It came to me quite suddenly, as it were out of the blue, and now that I look back on it, it seems to me that it was one of the decisive events of my life. Up to that time I had lived the life of a normal schoolboy, quite content with the world as I found it. Now I was suddenly made aware of another world of beauty and mystery such as I had never imagined to exist, except in poetry. It was as though I had begun to see and smell and hear for the first time. The world appeared to me as Wordsworth describes it with "the glory and the freshness of a dream." The sight of a wild rose growing on a hedge, the scent of lime tree blossoms caught suddenly as I rode down a hill on a bicycle, came to me like visitations from another world....I experienced an overwhelming emotion in the presence of nature, especially at evening. It began to wear a kind of sacramental character for me. I approached it with a sense of almost religious awe, and in the hush which comes before sunset, I felt again the presence of an unfathomable mystery.

Two boys, two innocents, gifted with a glimpse of the beyond. It surely must have been overwhelming for them, the evidence being that they never forgot the event.

I've been thinking more about Martin's and Griffiths's experience, actually I'm haunted by what happened to them, and all day I've wondered why I was. I felt as if I were trying to remember something from my past, something that had profoundly moved me when I was young. Yet I couldn't remember what it was until tonight when I was watching the setting sun.

When I was a teenager living in the city, I longed to live in the country. This longing was the result of my reading Henry David Thoreau's *Walden* and William Wordsworth's poetry, especially *The Prelude*. I hated the ugliness of urban life with its noise, its pollution, its overcrowding, and its lack of beauty. I longed to live in the country. And then, don't ask me how I found the book, I read Richard Jefferies's *The Story of My Soul*, a book that to this day remains one of my favorites. It reminds me of what both Martin and Griffiths experienced, for Jeffries too, when he was seventeen, was touched by divinity through the beauty of nature. Here is a brief sample of his writing, describing his longing for, what else could it be, God.

> Speaking by an inclination towards, not in words, my soul prays that I may have something from each of these, that I may gather a flower from them, that I have in myself the secret and meaning of the earth, the golden sun, the light, the foam-flecked sea. Let my soul become enlarged; I am not enough; I am little and contemptible. I desire a greatness of soul, an irradiance of mind, a deeper insight, a broader hope. Give me power of soul, so that I may actually effect by its will that which I strive for.

VII

It's now already January 4, 2011. I've had to abandon this diary in order to finish two books for my publisher. One of them concerns Thomas Merton; it will be my last book on Merton: I've had my say about Merton, and it's now time to let him go. The other is *Walking with Gerard Manley Hopkins.* I thought my fascination with Hopkins would be satisfied with my writing a novel about him, but when asked by my publisher to write a "walking with G. M. Hopkins," I quickly agreed (writing the book was a delight, but it was severely edited and censored). With both books now completed, I can return to Martin.

Coincidently this week Martin has a rather fine pre-Easter article in *America*, "Get Closer: Our desires for God come from God and lead us to the divine mystery." I've decided to make his article my Lenten meditation. It should take me well into Lent.

In his writing, Martin employs contemporary language, which, I believe, is the secret of his success as a writer on modern spirituality (he's even allowed by his Catholic publishers to use common swear words!). He avoids religious jargon, and speaks the talk heard in school, in college, in business, on the street, in homes, and so on. So to use the word *desire* in regard to God draws one in very quickly.

We talk a great deal today about desires: desires for sex, money, food, power, advancement, and so on. Here, however, he is juxtaposing desire with God. Let's face it, he argues, our greatest desire is for God. We want God in our lives. Some people are conscious of this desire; it's not an "obscure impulse": it's a fact of life. With other people, it's an unconscious impulse; therefore, they are people who haven't a clue as to why they're unhappy or lack peace of mind.

Martin says that there are several ways in which our desire for God is revealed. He chooses to write about three: Incompletion, Common Longings, and Vulnerability.

I must be candid: Although I subscribe to *America*, I don't often read it. If I do read anything in it, it's usually the book reviews, which tend to be quite fine, written by people who have the expertise to review books that fall within the purview of their field of knowledge. In other words, they at *America* carefully choose their reviewers, which is not always the case with newspapers and magazines.

I've read little of Martin in *America*. In fact, I can't even remember the last article of his I read. But this one on getting closer to God has me quite intrigued. My one cavil: he has a tendency to repeat himself, assuming that he must identify himself in every book he writes. Perhaps he's not aware of his widening reputation as a reputable commentator on American spirituality. Or he doesn't quite believe in it, and thus in his every book I've read thus far, he again introduces himself.

Martin comments on the issue of modern meaninglessness, one that is felt by many people throughout the world. Existentialism failed to explain away such a feeling, and as a philosophy, it offered no cure for it. One of Martin's strengths is that he knows pop culture, and he employs it to underscore his spiritual message. In his essay, he quotes from the singer Peggy Lee's popular hit song, "Is That All There Is?" I'm old enough to remember when this song came out. I also happen to know that Miss Lee fought to have the rights to sing the song first. It is a poignant song because the lyrics question a life devoid of meaning: Is that all there is? We are born, live and die, and that's it? The song's "answer" to such a bleak view of life is "to have a ball." That is, to party. Well, there are plenty of people actually doing it, but are they truly happy?

Martin identifies such a feeling about life as *Incompletion*. Such a feeling never really fades away forever. It's one of the reasons we continue to long for God. He again quotes St. Augustine's well-known comment, "Our hearts are restless until they rest in you." He adds that God uses our incompletion to draw us to him. It's a good argument (who would argue with Augustine?). I'm just impressed by Martin's willingness (and it is indeed risky) to refer to popular songs in his spiritual writing. He takes chances, and if what he really wants is to bring people closer to God, such risk taking is more than admirable—it's bold and courageous.

Modern man's sense of emptiness has not escaped our greatest thinkers. I think of Carl Jung and his book *Modern Man in Search of a Soul*. Martin calls this modern sense of emptiness by one of its popular names, a "God-shaped hole," one that only God can fill. His imagery also reminds me of Thomas Merton's fascination with the concept of the *pointe vierge*, that virgin point within our souls, a pure place always present and always virginal (pure) for our encounter with God. No matter how much we are alienated from God, that virgin point is forever waiting for our union with the divine.

During this season of Lent, I often reread Francis Thompson's *The Hound of Heaven*. He too believed, "All things betray thee, who betrayest Me." To betray God by sin is to allow that God-shaped hole within our souls to remain empty, and that sense of emptiness manifests itself in various fashions: restlessness, incompletion, anxiety, feelings of low self-esteem, anger, depression, in general, a lack of peace and happiness. The Good News is that we don't have to settle for that empty hole. We can easily fill it by returning to God. It's quite easy: all we have to do is pray. And the first prayer should be one of praise, the second, one of contrition, and the third, one of gratitude. Not impossibly difficult!

Martin understands the modern sensibility better than I. He writes about how today's men and women try to fill their emptiness, particularly by addictive behavior. He mentions drugs, alcohol, gambling, shopping, sexual addictions, and compulsive eating. He warns that addictions, if not quickly addressed, easily lead to greater problems: disintegration, loneliness, and despair. And, I would add, suicide.

One of the great tragedies of our time is the number of suicides of young people. As a teacher of young people, I knew several students who had taken their lives. I will never forget how shocked I was on learning about their deaths. My youth was not an easy one, but I knew I could always turn to God. Today's kids have nothing to turn to. Some think their music will save them, but in many cases, the music can't even save the composers of the music, for example, Kurt Cobain. Look at the mess of a Charlie Sheen, a tragedy in the making. His poor father Martin Sheen must be suffering; he is a practicing Catholic who has repeatedly tried to help his son, but to no avail.

Today's portion of Martin's essay concerns his comments on "Longing." He writes about those experiences that many of us feel, for example, becoming tearful at the sight of woods filling up with snow, or at a moving scene in a movie or play, or even at a church service. These experiences symbolize an inner longing for something totally Other—God. He tells the story of a woman, a lapsed Catholic, who at the baptism of a friend's child, began to weep. At first, she was completely surprised by her reaction, but at the same time, she felt an intense peace descend upon her, a peace she hadn't felt in many years. For Martin, just another example of a person who longs for God, a longing that often manifests itself when our defenses are *down.* This woman was caught off guard; her well-composed, modern mask fell off, and she felt the numinous for the first time in years, and she wept. She then tried to dismiss her reaction, as so many people do, as emotionality. We do anything rather than face the truth. T. S. Eliot says it best, that humankind cannot bear too much reality.

Martin speaks to her unwillingness to face the fact that she's frightened about having an intimate relationship with God. Why? Because it means *commitment*, and most people have difficulty with commitment: it means being faithful to a way of life, in this case, a Christian way of life, a life of emulating Jesus Christ. Not easy to do, but the fruits of such a Christ-centered life are plentiful and real.

I have to admit I am enjoying meditating on Martin's essay, perfect for Lent. Martin's comments are food for the soul. I'm also glad he's not referring to Ignatius of Loyola.

I am now on Martin's third way in which our desire for God is revealed: Vulnerability. Here he is addressing what we at one time described as foxhole faith. During wars, when soldiers are fighting (in World War I much of the fighting done from mud-hole trenches), they often turn to God because of fear of death. I've addressed vulnerability before: Is fear of imminent death a bad thing? Martin suggests no. He convincingly says where else is a man or woman going to turn with death staring him in the face? It's not a weakness, but in fact, it's a necessity. Vulnerability is nothing to be ashamed of, and if it returns us to God because we are in crisis, then so be it. The crisis may indeed be God's way of pulling us toward him, to paraphrase George Herbert.

Of the several famous World War I poets, it was its most famous poet, Siegfried Sassoon, who turned to God. But not while he was trapped in the trenches or soon after. He turned to God when he was an old man. To his family's dismay, he embraced the Roman Catholic Church, and for the first time in his life, he experienced peace of mind. He was greatly influenced by the contemplative nuns of Stanbrook Abbey, England. His late poetry is overtly religious, reminding me of George Herbert's metaphysical poetry. It is sad that his son has refused to allow his father's late spiritual verse to be included in his *Collected Poems.* I fear it may be a case of anger over his father's conversion to Rome, as indicated to me by a nun at Stanbrook. But it was not the trenches that turned him to God. It was Incompletion, Longing, and Vulnerability (manifested by old age and the approach of death).

In today's meditation on Vulnerability, I focused on Martin's story about the death of his father. Martin is very like Henri Nouwen in his willingness to share aspects of his personal life with his readers. His father had lost his job when he was in his fifties, and he had a difficult time finding another one. Then shortly afterward, he discovered he had cancer of the lungs that had quickly spread to his brain. It was a trying time for Martin and his family. His father, usually a hard and aloof man, changed. Illness had rendered him vulnerable, more vulnerable than he'd ever been before. The approach of death rather than embitter his father actually transformed him into a more feeling and spiritual man. He opened up to his family. He talked about God. He shared his newfound joy in prayer and held onto holy cards as if they were precious icons.

Martin was astonished by his father's transformation, for as a Catholic he had always been a lukewarm one, to say the least. In his vulnerability, being stripped of all that is worldly, all that we think is important, he faced life and death squarely in the face. And he was not found wanting. When Martin shared his amazement about the change in his father with a nun who had been one of his professors, she offered him an insightful observation, "Dying is about becoming more human."

I've been meditating all day on Martin's father's death. Death is the one reality about which we're all certain. It's the future of every human being. I used to be afraid of death, but that fear disappeared when I sat by my mother's bedside and watched her die of pneumonia. I hadn't realized how agonizing such a death pneumonia actually is. I had directed her doctor that no extraordinary means were to be employed to keep my mother alive if she became physically sick. She was in the last stages of profound dementia, and to all intents and purposes, she had long ago disappeared, not into death but into a death-like darkness.

Watching her struggle for breath, I writhed with her in her struggle. I held tightly onto her hand. The nurse saw me holding onto mother and said that I should go home, for my mother didn't even know I was present. I thought it was a rather insensitive comment because my mother was dying, and of course, I wanted to be with her. I would whisper to her about the past, "Remember this, Ma...." And the nurse, a gruff old nurse who long ago lost any sensitivity she may once have had, would say, "She doesn't hear you." The nursing profession after many years sometimes turns these good women into hardened people; it's a survival technique, and I understood it.

But to test whether or not my mother truly was "gone," I said, "Ma, if you know I'm here, squeeze my hand." And she squeezed it! I then knew my presence with her in her dying moments was important not only for me but for her. She wasn't gone, her humanity wasn't gone, her motherhood wasn't gone. She was still very much alive, but she was in agony, and I was beside her.

During this season of Lent, I of course can't help thinking of Jesus in the Garden of Gethsemane. He went off to pray by himself, an agonizing time for him, for like many a soldier at war or terminal patients in hospitals, he too knew his horrific death was approaching. And when he returned to his disciples, he found them all sleeping, and he was hurt. His humanity was hurt; he was *wounded* before one slash of the whip, before one thorn of the crown digging into his scalp, before the burden of the cross thrust upon his shoulder. Before any of that, there was no one in the Garden to share his pain, to remain awake with him.

Martin's friend said, "Dying is about becoming more human." I'd rather say, you don't become *more* human in dying, you simply *are* human: a person who dies every day of his life, until that final day when it actually occurs.

In the past, monks kept on their desks a skull to remind them of their mortality. We don't need skulls to remind us. Every time we look in the mirror, we should look closely. The face upon which you gaze will get old, it will become more wrinkled, the skin will lose its youthful color and gleam, the eyes will lose their luster, the brow will be furrowed more deeply depending on how harsh our lives (and our suffering) have been. Our faces are all we need to remind us of death, not a bare, human skull. To think in these terms is not morbid, because just recently I mentioned this very thought to someone, and I was accused of morbidity. I accused my friend of escapism: we *will* die. It doesn't have to be a morbid preoccupation: it is a fact of life, one we were reminded of at the beginning of Lent, on Ash Wednesday.

When I think of death, it paradoxically enhances my appreciation of my life. I'm instantly gladdened that I'm healthy (for now anyway), glad that I have my freedom, that I'm not trapped in a hospital room. Glad that I can travel, meet friends, in short, live. And I always try to remember Mary Oliver's poem "When Death Comes." In it, she expresses her hope that during her life she will remain a person married to amazement. Well, I too want to go through my life amazed by the world's wonder, beauty, and mystery. Like Henry David Thoreau, I hope that when I finally come to my death, I won't feel that I have not lived fully and richly, for to me, one of the greatest tragedies is to come to one's death and realize that one hadn't really lived at all. The novelist Henry James's greatest fear was that of the "unlived life."

Martin is on the mark: vulnerability is one of God's ways of drawing us near him, as happened with Martin's father.

How quickly Lent is passing by. Today I ran into an old friend I've not seen in a while. He's a pious man. I asked him if he was attending Mass every day of Lent. His reply was humbling, "I go to daily Mass, Lent or no Lent."

There was a time when I too attended daily Mass. I loved the little chapel of St. Teresa's Church not too far from my home. The beauty of the chapel, the intimacy of its smallness, the devotion of the priest celebrating the Mass, were all factors that drew me to attend. And the other attraction was that the Mass was late in the afternoon, ideal for a teacher. So at 4:00 p.m., I would be among about fifty people at Mass. Now that I think of it, I always felt better when I left Mass. It is a feeling I really can't put into words. I guess the word to describe my feeling is *ineffable*. I don't believe I could even obliquely describe it. It would be like describing love, another indescribable aspect of our lives, although there are innumerable words daily penned about love, to the point that we have cheapened the very word *love* so that "I love ice cream" is equated with "I love you."

I'm now approaching the end of Martin's article. I'm sad to have to leave it. Actually, I don't have to leave it, for I could easily reread it, and I would probably have another goodly number of meditations quite different from the ones I've written for this book.

His final thought is a simple one. Where do these feelings of Incompletion, Longing, and Vulnerability come from? He again reminds us that God *plants* these desires in our souls. Here again, we see the influence of Thomas Merton, who in his book *Seeds of Contemplation* says the very same words: God plants these *seeds* in us. It's up to us to water and nurture them so that they will grow and blossom. Yes, the responsibility is ours and no one else's. It's a *great* responsibility, and I regrettably have not always remembered this truth. It's the reason why the season of Lent is important for us spiritually: it reminds us of what truly is important in our life.

Today I have to have my car's oil changed—I'm scrupulously faithful to its timetable because my mechanic always places a sticker up in the corner of the window to remind me—and I follow his directions! It occurs to me that I've sometimes taken better care of my car than my soul, a good theme for my next Lenten meditation.

Conclusion

Dear Father Martin,

It's now spring, the crocuses are already gone, and I look forward to seeing my first robin and the blooming forsythia. And, of course, Easter is on the horizon, but it is now time to end my walk with you.

When my editor suggested I "walk" with you in another book, I was at first reluctant because I truly didn't know much about you. Except for a few essays I had read in *America*, I was totally unfamiliar with you or your books. But I'm now glad I allowed myself to be coaxed into our "walk."

The hook that convinced me that I had indeed made a good decision in writing *Walking with James Martin, SJ* was your tremendous admiration for Thomas Merton. You and I share a love for his life and his work. You credit him with your priestly vocation and claim him as your early spiritual mentor, long before you knew anything of Ignatius of Loyola, the founder of your order, the Society of Jesus. Thomas Merton was (remains) my spiritual mentor: I have turned to him most of my life when I needed spiritual direction and sustenance, and it has led to my penning five books about him.

As I read through your books, I soon realized, however, that your method and writing style was more like another of my most admired spiritual writers, Henri Nouwen. Like his, your writing possesses a transparency that Merton only rarely achieved because you are so willing to share your personal life with your readers; thus, we get to

113

know not only you and your struggles to become a priest but also your priestly journey. You seem not to be afraid to reveal the intimate side of your life, your friendships, your early ignorance of many Catholic rituals and prayers, and your hopes and dreams as a priest in our contemporary church. Although your opinions fall within the boundaries of church teaching, you will risk opinions that some may question, but because they are directly on the margin, nobody can accuse you of anything unorthodox. From a Jesuit, and let's face it, Jesuits usually play it safe, I find this writing refreshing.

While "walking" with you, I have achieved a better understanding of the Jesuit tradition. Your being a Jesuit actually made it an easier task for me to embrace this book because as a youngster I was an altar boy for the Jesuits of my parish in Boston. Most of the priests for whom I served Mass were academics teaching at either Boston College High School or Boston College. I will admit that they (the priests) were for the most part aloof. But one among them, the pastor of our church, I now believe was a mystic. I shall always remember serving his Masses. None of the other priests celebrated Mass with such reverence. Even the turning of the missal page was done deliberately as if he were indeed touching a relic. And at the consecration, to a little boy of twelve years, Father Robert Carr seemed to "disappear." I now believe he experienced spiritual union with Christ. If I had to describe why I feel this way, words would fail. It was the great writer William James who wrote that the mystic's experience was "ineffable." And so I must leave it at that.

Your life, it seems to me, illustrates the theme of one of my favorite poets, Francis Thompson, the author of "The Hound of Heaven." It seems that at first you did your best to elude your priestly vocation. But God is like a hound, and he would not give up on you until he indeed captured you. You yourself could claim Thompson's words,

I fled Him, down the nights and down the days;
   I fled Him, down the arches of the years;
I fled Him, down the labyrinthine ways
   Of my own mind; and in the mist of tears
I hid from Him, and under running laughter.
      Up vistaed hopes I sped;
      And shot, precipitated,
Adown Titanic glooms of chasmed fears,
   From those strong Feet that followed, followed after.
      But with unhurrying chase,
      And unperturbèd pace,
Deliberate speed, majestic instancy,
      They beat—and a Voice beat
      More instant than the Feet—
"All things betray thee, who betrayest Me."

Today we need spiritual writers who can communicate with our contemporaries. You don't live in an ivory tower. You are out there mingling among everyday people. Unlike your spiritual hero Thomas Merton, you have the privilege to not only write but to reach out to people through several media: radio, TV, the Internet, blogging, and, of course, your books. You're not afraid of our new technologies of communication; thus, in a short time, you have reached millions of Catholics and non-Catholics with your down-to-earth spiritual message. I say "down-to-earth" because yours is a message grounded in the incarnation, that Christ was indeed both Person and Divine. Too often we Catholics forget that Christ became man for us; thus, he experienced *all* that we experience (except sin), and thus we should never be afraid to turn to him: he is always ready to receive us "without blame" as the poet George Herbert reminds us in his beautiful poem "Love Bade Me Welcome."

I read of your book about your ministry at Ground Zero on 9/11. For me it was a painful book to read. You so sensitively and beautifully wrote about your experience during this tragic time. How exquisitely you dealt with everyone; how your humanity reached out to so many. At that time, you were at your best as a man and as a priest. I hope I'm not sounding presumptuous in saying this, but I say it humbly and from the bottom of my heart.

So it is now time to say farewell. But not forever, for I shall carry in my heart your message: And is not the message of Christ summed up in one word, Love? Well, it's your message too, as it should be, of course, you a member of the Society of Jesus.

Blessings,
Robert Waldron